Pathological Demand Avoidance & Autism

Essential Education for Parents, Educators & Family about PDA in ASD: Behavioral Strategies for Supporting & Managing Neurodiversity

Erica May

used for personal use. Furthermore, it should not be shared with any other individual or persons for any purpose other than that for which it was initially intended. It is strictly prohibited to amend, reproduce, distribute, utilize, quote, or paraphrase any part of the content within this publication without prior authorization from the writer or publisher. Any violation of these regulations may result in legal action against those who have breached them.

Disclaimer Notice

The presented work is strictly informational and should not be interpreted as an offer to buy or sell any form of security, instrument, or investment vehicle. Furthermore, the information contained herein should not be taken as a medical, legal, tax, accounting, or investment recommendation given by the author(s) or any affiliated company, employees, or paid contributors. In other words, the information is presented without considering individual preferences for specific investments in terms of risk parameters. It is general information that does not account for a person's lifestyle and financial objectives. It is important to note that no tailored advice will be provided based on the given information.

Table Of Contents

PREFACE 15

Embarking on a Journey of Understanding: A Guide to Pathological Demand Avoidance (PDA) 15

INTRODUCTION 18

CHAPTER 1: DECODING THE MYSTERY OF PDA ... 21

When Anxiety Wears a Disguise 21

Understanding Pathological Demand Avoidance (PDA): A Unique Profile within the Autism Spectrum 25

Grasping the Underlying Causes of PDA 27

CHAPTER 2: INSIDE THE MIND OF PDA: UNDERSTANDING ANXIETY AND AVOIDANCE 31

Peering Through the Veil of Avoidance 31

Practical Strategies for Managing These Behaviors Include: 35

Navigating Sensory Processing and Emotional Regulation Challenges in Individuals with Pathological Demand Avoidance (PDA) 36

CHAPTER 3: TAILORING STRATEGIES: CRAFTING AN INDIVIDUALIZED SUPPORT PLAN 41

Unveiling the Art of Individualized Support in PDA 41

Step-by-Step Process: "Pathway to Personalization" 43

Step 1: Review different approaches to supporting individuals with PDA43

Step 2: Discover tailored interventions for PDA's complex needs 43

Step 3: Learn to develop a customizable support plan 44

Crafting Tailored Interventions for Individuals with Pathological Demand Avoidance (PDA) 46

Tailoring an Individualized Support Plan for PDA 48

Identifying Strengths and Interests 49

Comprehensive Assessment 49

Collaborative Goal Setting 49

Intervention Planning 50

Flexible Implementation 50

Evaluation and Reflection 50

Emphasis on Autonomy and Relationships 51

CHAPTER 4: THE LANGUAGE OF SUPPORT: USING DECLARATIVE LANGUAGE AND CHOICE 53

Transforming Challenges into Opportunities: Mastering Declarative Language and Choice in PDA 53

Step-by-Step Guide: Crafting Calm 55

Step 1: Master the Art of Declarative Language 55

Step 2: Understand the Power of Choice Offering 55

Step 3: Identify Early Signs of Anxiety and Employ Strategies to Prevent Escalation 56

Empowering Through Choices: Supporting Individuals with Pathological Demand Avoidance (PDA) 58

CHAPTER 5: SENSORY-FRIENDLY ENVIRONMENTS AND SELF-REGULATION 63

Harnessing Harmony: Crafting Calm Spaces for Unique Minds 63

Step 1: Implement Sensory-Friendly Strategies 65

Step 2: Utilize Mindfulness and Other Techniques for Self-Regulation 65

Step 3: Create Supportive Environments for Better Self-Management of Anxiety 66

Cultivating Self-Regulation: Mindfulness and Techniques for Individuals with Pathological Demand Avoidance (PDA) 68

Sensory Integration and Self-Regulation Framework 70

CHAPTER 6: UNVEILING PDA: FROM MISUNDERSTANDING TO MASTERY 74

Peeling Back the Layers of PDA 74

Tailoring Support Strategies for Individuals with Pathological Demand Avoidance (PDA) 78

CHAPTER 7: VOICES OF PDA: HOW DOES PDA MANIFEST IN REAL LIFE? 84

Unmasking the Everyday: Insights into PDA 84

Navigating Real-Life Examples: Strategies for Managing Pathological Demand Avoidance (PDA) Behaviors 88

CHAPTER 8: NAVIGATING THE RESOURCES LANDSCAPE FOR PDA SUPPORT 93

Unlocking Support: Essential Tools and Communities for PDA 93

Empowering Resources for Diagnosing and Assessing Pathological Demand Avoidance (PDA) 97

Online Screening Tools 97

Diagnostic Criteria Checklist 98

Behavioral Observation Tools 98

Communication Skills Assessment 98

Sensory Processing Tools 99
Collaborative Evaluation Frameworks 99
Multidisciplinary Assessment Approaches 100

CHAPTER 9: ACTIONABLE INSIGHTS: IMPLEMENTING STRATEGIES THROUGH CHECKLISTS AND TEMPLATES 105

Transforming Insight into Action 105

Crafting Personalized Action Plans for Supporting Individuals with Pathological Demand Avoidance (PDA) 109

Action Implementation Framework: Navigating Support Strategies for Individuals with PDA 111
Current Situation Evaluation 111
SMART Goal Setting 111
Action Plan Development 112
Monitoring Progress 112
Reflection and Iteration 113
Application Scenarios 113

CHAPTER 10: CLARIFYING QUESTIONS: EXPERT ANSWERS TO COMMON PDA QUERIES 116

Are You Navigating the Complexities of PDA? Get Expert Answers Now 116

Dispelling Myths and Understanding Realities of Pathological Demand Avoidance (PDA) 120

CHAPTER 11: A COMPASSIONATE APPROACH: STRATEGIES FOR SIBLINGS AND PEERS 126

Empathy in Action: Supporting Siblings and Peers 126

Fostering Inclusive Relationships and Compassion in Family and Peer Circles 130

CHAPTER 12: THE CAREGIVER'S JOURNEY: SELF-CARE AND EMOTIONAL SUPPORT..........................136

When the Caregiver Needs Care 136

Cultivating Resilience and Finding Support in Caregiving.................140

CHAPTER 13: ADVOCACY AND AWARENESS: NAVIGATING SOCIAL AND LEGAL LANDSCAPES 145

Shaping the Future Through Understanding and Action 145

Navigating Legal Considerations and Educational Rights for Individuals with PDA...149

CHAPTER 14: LOOKING AHEAD: THE FUTURE OF PDA RESEARCH AND SUPPORT...........................155

Envisioning Tomorrow: The Evolution of PDA Insight and Intervention 155

Joining Support Networks and Communities for Understanding and Growth 159

EPILOGUE 164

Embracing the Journey: A Closing Reflection............................164

CONCLUSION 168

BONUS MATERIAL 171

Your Questions, Answered!...**171**

1. How Can Parents Initially Identify Signs of PDA in Their Children? 171

2. What Are the Key Differences Between PDA and Other Forms of Autism? 173

3. How Can Teachers Adapt Classroom Environments to Better Support Students With Pda?... 175

4. What Strategies Can Professionals Employ to Encourage Cooperation From Individuals With PDAs without Triggering Their Demand Avoidance?.. 177

5. What Role Do Genetics and Environment Play in the Development of PDA? 179

6. How Can Families Advocate for the Needs of a Member With PDA within the Broader Community or School System?........................ 181

7. What Are the Most Effective Therapeutic Approaches for Managing PDA, and How Do They Differ From Those Used With Other Asd Conditions?.. 183

8. Can Adults Be Diagnosed With PDA, and if So, How Does the Diagnostic Process Differ From That for Children?....................... 185

9. How Does Pda Affect Social Relationships and Friendships, and What Strategies Can Help Foster Positive Interactions?................. 187

10. What Are the Long-Term Outlooks for Individuals With PDA in Terms of Independence, Employment, and Quality of Life?............ 189

11. How Can Siblings of Individuals With Pda Understand and Cope With the Unique Challenges Their Family Faces?........................... 191

12. In What Ways Can Technology Be Leveraged to Assist Individuals With PDA in Learning and Communication?................ 193

13. Are There Specific Legal Protections or Accommodations Individuals With PDA Can or Should Receive in the Educational System or Workplace? 195

14. How Can Stress and Mental Health Challenges That Often Accompany PDA be Effectively Managed for Both the Individual and Their Families? 197

15. What Ongoing Research is Being Conducted on PDA, and How Might It Change the Understanding or Treatment of the Condition in the Future? 199

Welcome to the

Ideas Worth Sharing

Series

My name is Nicholas Bright, and I've spent nearly two decades working as a psychologist specializing in Behavioral Neuroscience and Interpersonal Communication in the US, UK, and Australia. Throughout my career, I've encountered countless stories, experiences, and insights that have shaped my understanding of the human mind and interpersonal interactions.

This series is a collaborative effort, bringing together the experience and expertise of myself and my colleagues: Erica May, Jeff Sharpe, Camila Alvarez, and potentially new faces in the future! We've chosen to write under pen names to respect everyone's privacy and keep the spotlight on the valuable content we offer rather than us as individuals. This decision allows us to freely share our knowledge without the distractions that often come with the limelight. We stand by the authenticity and credibility of the content shared here—our professional integrity remains at the forefront of this series.

We are deeply passionate about our field, and our primary goal is to equip you with practical, research-backed insights that you can implement in your everyday life. Each chapter is designed to inspire and help you better understand yourself and those around you.

We invite you to engage actively with the material: take notes, discuss the ideas with friends and family, and, most importantly, apply the lessons in your daily routine.

1. **Read;** understand what can be done to improve
2. **Reflect;** appreciate your feelings and their origins
3. **Remember;** put your learning into action

Thank you for embarking on this journey of knowledge and growth with us,

Nick

Want to Win Free Books?

Join Our Newsletter!

In this series, we appreciate that someone may find many different books helpful. I certainly know that when discussing sensitive topics like, for example, divorce, we can end up working on grief, anxiety, self-confidence, cognitive dissonance, and lots more. When we encounter a major challenge in life, it is rarely due to one small problem but rather a concoction of our experiences, outlooks, and actions; it's often a deep-rooted issue with many different things we need to uncover and support. We are complicated beings, and we must recognize this. As such, I would love to invite you all to join our newsletter.

In this, I aim to write articles of interest, including excerpts from various books in the series, as well as **vouchers, discounts**, and **giveaways**—and of course, no gimmicks or catches. I harbor a deep loathing of companies that offer seemingly amazing deals, only to charge you vast amounts in hidden fees! I vowed to never fall into that trap myself, and any offers I make are designed to be of true benefit and help. If you win a book in a giveaway, I want you to read it with a smile.

Join our newsletter and discover the additional value we can add to your life's curriculum!

Join us at: **www.IdeasWorthSharingSeries.com/newsletter**

See you on the inside!

About the Author: Dr. Erica May

Dr Erica May is a dedicated Clinical Psychologist practising in New York City. She graduated from Syracuse University in New York State, earning her degree in Clinical Psychology. Erica specializes in Cognitive Behavioral Therapy (CBT), Dialectical Behavior Therapy (DBT), and trauma-focused treatments. Her work is deeply rooted in helping individuals navigate complex emotional landscapes, enabling them to lead healthier and more fulfilling lives. Her compassionate approach and expertise have garnered her a reputation as a trusted mental health professional in her local community.

Erica has been friends and has worked with Nicholas Bright, the lead author of the Ideas Worth Sharing series, for many years. Together, they aim to help support a wider community by writing a book series on important topics within Psychology and extending their therapeutic insights and techniques beyond the confines of their practice. This book series will cover various topics related to mental health, including detailed guides on implementing CBT and DBT strategies in daily life, as well as comprehensive approaches to prevention, understanding and healing. By presenting practical exercises and learning through her practice, Erica hopes to make evidence-based psychological concepts more accessible to a broader audience. She aims to empower individuals with the knowledge and tools to manage their mental health proactively and independently, fostering greater resilience and well-being.

Preface

"The only real mistake is the one from

which we learn nothing."

Henry Ford

Embarking on a Journey of Understanding: A Guide to Pathological Demand Avoidance (PDA)

Navigating the multifaceted world of Pathological Demand Avoidance (PDA), a lesser-known profile within the autism spectrum presents unique challenges and profound opportunities for growth and understanding. This book is a comprehensive guide crafted to demystify PDAs and furnish parents, educators, and therapists with actionable strategies to support those under their care. Our journey through these pages will explore how individuals with PDA perceive and interact with their world, emphasizing practical solutions that respect their distinct needs.

The decision to write this book stemmed from numerous conversations with overwhelmed parents and professionals who felt ill-equipped to manage the complexities of PDAs. These discussions highlighted a critical gap in accessible resources that explain what PDA is and how to respond to its manifestations effectively. Through this work, I aim to bridge this gap, providing clarity and confidence to those who feel lost in the sea of generalized autism advice that often fails to address the specificities of PDA.

This book is shaped by insights from leading experts in autism and PDA, as well as the real-world experiences of individuals living with PDA and their families. It is also a product of extensive research and collaboration with professionals across multiple disciplines who have generously shared their knowledge and time.

I am deeply grateful to you, the reader, for choosing to embark on this enlightening journey with me. Your commitment to understanding and supporting individuals with PDA is a decisive step toward fostering a more inclusive and empathetic world.

This guide is designed for those directly involved in caring for or educating someone with a PDA. Whether you are a parent grappling with daily challenges, an educator seeking effective classroom strategies, or a therapist refining your approach to therapy, you will find valuable insights and practical tools within these pages.

Thank you for your trust in selecting this book. As we turn each page together, I invite you to engage actively with the strategies discussed, applying them to your unique situations. Let us move beyond mere awareness towards mastery and empathy, transforming challenges into opportunities for growth and connection. Your journey through understanding PDA deeply starts now; let's embrace it together with open hearts and minds.

Introduction

"The beauty of the world lies in the

diversity of its people."

Unknown

Navigating the complex world of neurodiversity can often feel like an intricate dance that requires empathy, understanding, and a deep respect for the unique rhythms of each individual. Within this vast spectrum, pathological demand avoidance (PDA) emerges as a profile that presents challenges and opportunities. It stretches the boundaries of our understanding and demands that we approach it with a fresh perspective that embraces flexibility over rigidity and understanding over dictation.

At the heart of this exploration is a simple yet profound recognition: individuals with PDA possess unique strengths and needs that must be acknowledged and respected. Their experiences, far from mere footnotes in the broader narrative of neurodiversity, shine a light on the incredible diversity of the human condition. These experiences invite us to question traditional models of behavior and support, urging us towards more nuanced and empathetic approaches.

This book is born out of a desire to bridge the gap between the rich, complex lives of individuals with PDA and the often narrow perceptions surrounding them. It seeks to provide a comprehensive look into what it means to live with or support someone with PDA. From unraveling the fabric of demand avoidance to exploring the emotional landscapes navigated by these individuals, the contents are crafted to offer insight, understanding, and practical advice.

Through a combination of scientific research, expert insights, and real-life stories, this narrative aims to offer a multidimensional view of PDA. It acknowledges the struggles and celebrates the triumphs, recognizing that within every challenge lies an opportunity for growth and understanding. This book does not claim all the answers but instead positions itself as a guide, a starting point for deeper exploration and discussion.

The importance of community and support networks cannot be overstressed. It becomes evident that the path to understanding and assisting individuals with PDA is not one to be walked alone. The shared journeys of families, educators, and professionals underscore the need for a collective approach that harnesses the power of shared knowledge and experiences to foster an environment of mutual learning and support.

At its core, this narrative champions hope, resilience, and empowerment principles. These are not abstract ideals but tangible practices that illuminate the path forward. They remind us that, despite the challenges, every individual with PDA has a wellspring of potential waiting to be recognized and nurtured.

Drawing upon these themes, the reader can intellectually, emotionally, and practically engage with the material. It's a call to action, urging the adoption of strategies that respect individuality and promote understanding. It's an encouragement to view every interaction as an opportunity to make a positive impact, no matter how small.

In crafting this introduction, the aim has been to set the stage for what is not merely an academic discussion but a profoundly personal exploration of what it means to live with, support, and love someone with PDA. It's an invitation to join a community of those who seek not just to understand but to make a difference in the lives of individuals with this unique profile.

As this journey begins, remember that the path to understanding and support is ongoing and evolving. Each chapter builds upon the last, weaving together theory, practice, and heart. Welcome to a conversation about PDA that goes beyond the surface, reaching into the essence of connecting, supporting, and thriving together.

Chapter 1: Decoding the Mystery of PDA

"Understanding is deeper than knowledge. There are

many people who know you, but very

few who understand you."

Nicholas Cage

When Anxiety Wears a Disguise

Pathological Demand Avoidance (PDA) is not merely about being stubborn or willful; it's a complex and deeply misunderstood profile within the autism spectrum. This condition is marked by an individual's intense aversion to everyday demands and expectations, which stems from overwhelming anxiety rather than simple non-compliance. For those living with PDA or supporting someone who does, understanding this fundamental distinction is essential. It opens the door to compassionate support strategies that recognize the unique challenges faced by these individuals.

At its core, PDA is characterized by extreme levels of anxiety triggered by what most would consider everyday demands—from wearing specific clothing to completing homework. This anxiety manifests in behaviors that are often perceived as manipulative or controlling but are, in fact, coping mechanisms for the intense distress these demands provoke. Recognizing these signs and understanding their root causes is crucial for effective interaction and support.

Distinguishing PDA from other forms of autism is vital, as traditional approaches to autism can prove ineffective or even counterproductive. Unlike other profiles on the spectrum where structured routines and clear expectations might be beneficial, individuals with PDA require flexibility and adaptability. Their need to control their environment and avoid demands can lead to significant challenges in educational settings, social interactions, and personal development.

Current research into PDA is shedding light on its underlying causes and refining diagnostic criteria. It's becoming clear that standard diagnostic frameworks for autism don't fully encompass the subtleties of PDA. This has led to misdiagnosis or underdiagnosis, leaving many without appropriate support. By delving into expert opinions and the latest studies, we can begin to map out more effective diagnostic tools and intervention strategies.

The importance of accurate diagnosis cannot be overstated—it's the gateway to understanding and support. With a proper understanding of PDA, parents, educators, and therapists can develop strategies that truly meet the needs of these individuals. These strategies are about managing behavior and creating environments where people with PDAs can thrive.

This chapter sets the stage for exploring practical solutions for supporting individuals with PDAs. We'll look at how to adapt educational approaches, foster social inclusion, and manage personal relationships effectively. By embracing a flexible mindset and focusing on individual strengths, we can transform challenges into opportunities for growth.

Understanding PDA is more than managing difficulties; recognizing and nurturing potential. As we continue through this book, remember that each strategy or insight builds towards creating a supportive framework that respects the unique ways people with PDA experience the world. Together, we'll discover how shifts in perspective and approach can make all the difference in helping these remarkable minds shine.

Pathological Demand Avoidance (PDA) is a unique profile within the autism spectrum that presents distinctive characteristics. Individuals with PDA experience extreme levels of anxiety in response to expectations and demands, leading to avoidant behaviors, manipulation, and control mechanisms. It is crucial to understand that these responses stem from overwhelming anxiety rather than mere defiance. This key differentiation is essential for developing empathetic support strategies that cater to the specific needs of individuals with PDAs.

One of the hallmark features of PDA is the individual's pervasive need to avoid everyday demands and requests. This avoidance stems from a deep-seated fear of failure or criticism, which can trigger overwhelming anxiety responses. Unlike typical defiance, which may arise from a desire for control or opposition, individuals with PDAs are driven by an intense need to protect themselves from perceived threats to their well-being. This distinction is critical in recognizing the underlying motivations behind their behavior.

Furthermore, individuals with PDA often display highly adaptive social communication skills when not under pressure. Their ability to engage effectively in social interactions can mask their difficulties coping with demands. This paradoxical behavior can lead to misconceptions about their capabilities and needs, making it challenging for others to understand the depth of their struggles.

Individuals with PDA may employ various strategies such as negotiating, distracting, or creating elaborate excuses to avoid tasks or demands. These strategies serve as coping mechanisms to manage their anxiety and regain a sense of control over their environment. Understanding these coping mechanisms can help caregivers and support networks provide tailored assistance that addresses the root cause of the avoidance behavior.

Recognizing the distinct characteristics of PDA is essential for creating supportive environments that nurture individuals with this profile. By acknowledging the anxiety-driven nature of their avoidance behaviors, caregivers and educators can develop strategies that focus on reducing stressors and providing alternative ways for individuals with PDA to engage with tasks and expectations. This approach shifts the focus from compliance to collaboration, fostering a more positive and empowering dynamic between individuals with PDAs and their support network.

Understanding Pathological Demand Avoidance (PDA): A Unique Profile within the Autism Spectrum

Pathological Demand Avoidance (PDA) stands out as a unique profile within the autism spectrum, characterized by extreme anxiety in response to expectations and demands. It is essential to distinguish PDA from other autism spectrum disorders to comprehend its distinct challenges fully. Unlike typical defiance or disobedience, individuals with PDA exhibit avoidant behaviors, manipulation, and control mechanisms as a response to overwhelming anxiety, not willful resistance. This crucial differentiation sets the stage for developing effective support strategies tailored to the specific needs of those with PDAs.

Understanding the unique challenges of PDA involves recognizing that traditional approaches to autism may not always be suitable. Individuals with PDA often struggle with everyday tasks and routines due to their intense anxiety surrounding demands. While some may mistake these behaviors for intentional defiance, it is vital to grasp that they stem from an internal struggle with overwhelming anxiety rather than a desire to be noncompliant. By acknowledging this distinction, caregivers, educators, and support systems can tailor their interactions and interventions accordingly.

One key aspect that sets PDA apart is the need for flexibility in expectations and approaches. Unlike some other autism spectrum disorders where predictability and routine are beneficial, individuals with PDA may find these structures stifling and anxiety-inducing. By allowing for more flexibility in routines and expectations, caregivers can help reduce the anxiety levels in individuals with PDA and create a more supportive environment for them to thrive.

Another distinctive challenge of PDA lies in recognizing the underlying anxiety driving avoidant behaviors. While it may appear as defiance on the surface, these behaviors are often protective mechanisms against overwhelming feelings of anxiety. Empathy and understanding play crucial roles in supporting individuals with PDA, as they help create a safe space where they feel heard and validated in their struggles.

Effective communication strategies are also essential when working with individuals with PDAs. Clear, concise instructions delivered in a non-confrontational manner can help reduce anxiety levels and facilitate better cooperation. By building trust and rapport, caregivers can establish strong relationships that form the foundation for successful interventions and support systems.

In navigating the complexities of PDA, it is vital to approach each individual with empathy and understanding, recognizing that their behaviors stem from a place of profound anxiety rather than intentional defiance. By tailoring support strategies to address the unique challenges of PDA, caregivers can create environments that promote growth, development, and emotional well-being for individuals living with this profile within the autism spectrum.

Grasping the Underlying Causes of PDA

Understanding the underlying causes of Pathological Demand Avoidance (PDA) is crucial in providing adequate support and intervention strategies for individuals with this unique profile within the autism spectrum. Research and expert opinions shed light on the complexity of PDA, highlighting the necessity to address its root causes rather than merely treating its symptoms.

One key aspect that experts point to is the extreme levels of anxiety experienced by individuals with PDA in response to expectations and demands. This anxiety can manifest as avoidant behaviors, manipulation, and control mechanisms, all aimed at alleviating the overwhelming stress triggered by demands. By recognizing that these behaviors stem from a place of deep anxiety rather than defiance, caregivers and professionals can tailor their approaches with empathy and understanding.

Moreover, sensory processing differences play a significant role in exacerbating anxiety levels in individuals with PDA. Sensory overload or sensory-seeking behaviors can intensify feelings of overwhelm and lead to avoidance strategies as a coping mechanism. Creating environments that account for sensory sensitivities can help reduce anxiety levels and provide a more supportive setting for individuals with PDA.

Neurological factors also contribute to the challenges faced by individuals with PDA. Differences in brain function related to processing demands, regulating emotions, and managing stress can impact how individuals respond to expectations. Recognizing these neurological differences is essential in developing tailored strategies that address the specific needs of individuals with PDA.

In addition to these factors, social communication difficulties inherent in autism spectrum disorders can further complicate interactions for individuals with PDA. Challenges in understanding social cues, expressing needs effectively, and navigating social relationships can contribute to increased anxiety levels when faced with demands from others.

By delving into the underlying causes of PDA, caregivers, educators, and professionals can gain a deeper insight into the unique challenges faced by individuals with this profile. This understanding paves the way for targeted interventions that address the behavioral manifestations of PDA and the root causes driving these behaviors. Empathy, patience, and a comprehensive approach considering all PDA aspects are essential in effectively supporting individuals with this complex profile.

Understanding Pathological Demand Avoidance (PDA) is the first step towards transforming challenges into opportunities for growth and support. This chapter has laid a solid foundation by clarifying what PDA is, how it differs from other conditions within the autism spectrum, and delving into the underlying causes and the latest research. Each of these points is crucial as they equip you with the knowledge to recognize and effectively respond to PDA, fostering a supportive environment that caters to unique needs.

Recognizing the distinctive characteristics of PDA is not just about identification; it's about beginning to see the world through a different lens—a lens that appreciates the intense anxiety that drives the avoidance behaviors seen in PDA. With this understanding, you are better prepared to offer empathy and tailored support rather than compliance-based strategies that often fail to meet their needs.

Moreover, distinguishing PDA from other autism spectrum disorders illuminates its unique challenges. This differentiation is vital as it guides caregivers, educators, and clinicians in crafting practical and respectful approaches to the individual's intrinsic need for autonomy and control. Understanding these nuances allows you to avoid common pitfalls in support strategies that might otherwise exacerbate anxiety or disengagement.

Lastly, grasping the underlying causes and staying informed about ongoing research empowers you with cutting-edge knowledge that can dramatically improve intervention approaches. It ensures that the support provided is based on the latest understanding of PDA, thereby increasing its effectiveness and relevance.

As we progress in this book, each chapter will build upon this foundation with practical strategies and real-world insights. You will learn how to create environments that reduce demand-induced anxiety, techniques for engaging cooperatively with individuals who have PDA, and methods to foster resilience and independence.

By equipping yourself with this knowledge and these skills, you are taking a significant step toward making a meaningful difference in the lives of those affected by PDAs. This journey will enhance your understanding and enable you to contribute to their well-being and success actively. The road ahead is promising, filled with opportunities for empowerment and transformation—both for you and for those you support or care about who navigate life with PDA.

Chapter 2: Inside the Mind of PDA: Understanding Anxiety and Avoidance

"Flexibility is the key to stability."

John Wooden

Peering Through the Veil of Avoidance

Pathological Demand Avoidance (PDA) represents a complex enigma within the autism spectrum, characterized by an intense avoidance of everyday demands and expectations. This avoidance is not born out of mere defiance. Still, it is rooted deeply in extreme anxiety—individuals with PDA experience a world where the ordinary feels overwhelming and fraught with insurmountable challenges. To understand and support someone with PDA, it's crucial to recognize how their attempts to control their environment stem from a need to manage this profound anxiety.

PDA's heart lies a tangled web of sensory processing difficulties and emotional regulation challenges. These individuals perceive sensory input differently, making typical environments hostile or unbearable. Imagine the hum of fluorescent lights sounding like a blaring siren or the gentle touch of a cotton shirt feeling akin to sandpaper. Such sensory discrepancies can escalate anxiety, leading to what might be perceived as irrational behaviors. Understanding these sensory triggers is the first step in creating supportive environments that mitigate rather than exacerbate stressors.

Moreover, emotional regulation in individuals with PDAs is a battlefield of its own. The emotional responses can be unpredictable and disproportionate, complicating interactions with others and the ability to cope with daily life. It's not just about managing tantrums or meltdowns; it's about understanding that these are manifestations of internal chaos they struggle to control. Here, the goal is to equip these individuals with strategies that help effectively modulate their emotional responses.

Social communication presents another layer of complexity for those with PDAs. They might find it challenging to interpret social cues or engage in reciprocal conversation, leading to misunderstandings and social isolation. The nuances of body language, tone of voice, and facial expressions that typically convey so much about a person's feelings and intentions are often lost on individuals with PDA. Developing tailored communication strategies that cater to their unique needs can significantly improve their social interactions and relationships.

To truly support someone with a PDA, one must adopt an approach that goes beyond conventional methods. Traditional behavioral techniques designed for other forms of autism spectrum disorders may not be effective for those with PDA due to their high anxiety levels and need for control over their environment. Instead, approaches that prioritize understanding and flexibility have proven more successful. This includes creating low-demand environments where choices are plentiful and pressures are minimal.

Practical strategies such as using indirect language or presenting tasks as games can also reduce perceived demands, thereby minimizing anxiety and avoidance behaviors. It's about making the individual feel safe enough to engage without feeling overwhelmed by expectations.

Empowering caregivers and educators through knowledge and practical tools is essential for fostering environments where individuals with PDA can thrive. By addressing sensory sensitivities, aiding emotional regulation, and enhancing communication skills, we pave the way for these unique minds to navigate life's demands more successfully.

Ultimately, embracing a compassionate approach that respects their need for autonomy while gently guiding them toward greater functionality can transform lives for individuals with PDAs and those around them who seek to understand and support them effectively.

Individuals with Pathological Demand Avoidance (PDA) often exhibit extreme anxiety that manifests in avoidant behaviors, manipulation, and control mechanisms. These behaviors can be challenging to navigate for caregivers, educators, and therapists trying to support individuals with PDAs. Avoidant behaviors may include refusal to engage in tasks or activities, excessive negotiation or bargaining to avoid demands, or even outright defiance in the face of perceived threats. Manipulation tactics might involve distraction techniques, creating chaos to divert attention, or using charm and persuasion to sidestep responsibilities. Control mechanisms can range from rigid routines and rituals to outright aggression when feeling overwhelmed.

Understanding these manifestations of extreme anxiety is crucial in effectively supporting individuals with PDA. By recognizing the underlying fear and distress driving these behaviors, caregivers and professionals can tailor strategies that address the root cause rather than just managing the outward symptoms. It's essential to approach these behaviors with empathy and a deep understanding of the intense anxiety that individuals with PDA experience in demanding situations. By acknowledging the anxiety behind avoidant behaviors, manipulation, and control mechanisms, caregivers can create environments that foster trust and cooperation.

Practical Strategies for Managing These Behaviors Include:

Providing clear choices: Offering individuals with PDAs a sense of control by presenting options within boundaries can help alleviate anxiety and reduce avoidance.

Using visual supports: Visual schedules, timers, and prompts can aid in clarifying expectations and reducing uncertainty.

Employing humor and creativity: Finding ways to inject humor and creativity into tasks can make them more engaging and less threatening for individuals with PDAs.

Implementing calm-down strategies: Teaching coping mechanisms such as deep breathing exercises or sensory tools can help regulate emotions during moments of high anxiety.

By implementing these strategies with empathy and consistency, caregivers can create supportive environments that empower individuals with PDA to manage their anxieties effectively. Recognizing the signs of extreme anxiety behind avoidant behaviors, manipulation tactics, and control mechanisms is the first step towards building trust and collaboration with individuals who face these challenges daily.

Navigating Sensory Processing and Emotional Regulation Challenges in Individuals with Pathological Demand Avoidance (PDA)

Individuals with Pathological Demand Avoidance (PDA) often experience significant sensory processing and emotional regulation challenges. These difficulties can manifest in various ways, impacting their daily lives and interactions. Sensory processing issues can lead to hypersensitivity or hyposensitivity to stimuli, making everyday experiences overwhelming or underwhelming for individuals with PDA. This heightened sensitivity can trigger anxiety and avoidance behaviors as a coping mechanism to manage the sensory overload they experience.

Understanding and addressing these sensory processing difficulties is crucial in supporting individuals with PDA. Caregivers, educators, and therapists can create environments that accommodate sensory needs by providing options for sensory breaks, using calming tools like noise-canceling headphones or weighted blankets, and minimizing sensory triggers when possible. By recognizing the unique sensory profiles of individuals with PDA and tailoring interventions accordingly, it becomes easier to help them navigate their surroundings with less distress.

Emotional regulation challenges are also prevalent among individuals with PDA, who may struggle to express, identify, or manage their emotions effectively. This can lead to outbursts, meltdowns, or shutdowns when emotions become overwhelming. Teaching emotional literacy through visual supports, social stories, and emotion regulation techniques can empower individuals with PDAs to constructively recognize and communicate their feelings. Providing a safe space for emotional expression and offering tools for self-regulation are essential strategies in helping individuals with PDA navigate their emotions more effectively.

It is vital to approach emotional regulation challenges with empathy and patience, acknowledging that individuals with PDA may need additional support learning how to regulate their emotions. By creating a supportive environment that fosters emotional awareness and provides coping mechanisms for managing intense feelings, caregivers and educators can help individuals with PDA build resilience and emotional competence over time.

In summary, addressing sensory processing and emotional regulation challenges is vital in supporting individuals with PDA. By implementing tailored strategies that accommodate sensory needs and promote emotional literacy, caregivers, educators, and therapists can empower individuals with PDAs to navigate their anxieties more effectively and engage with the world around them in a more manageable way. Understanding the impact of sensory processing and emotional regulation on individuals with PDA makes it possible to create supportive environments that promote growth, self-expression, and overall well-being.

Individuals with Pathological Demand Avoidance (PDA) often

face significant social communication barriers that can hinder their interactions with others. These barriers may manifest as difficulties in understanding social cues, initiating and maintaining conversations, and struggles with empathy and perspective-taking. Caregivers, educators, and therapists must recognize these obstacles and implement strategies to help individuals with PDA navigate the complexities of social interactions effectively.

One key strategy to overcome social communication barriers in PDA individuals is providing clear and explicit instructions. Ambiguity or vague language can lead to confusion and anxiety for individuals with PDA, making it harder for them to engage in social exchanges. Caregivers can help alleviate uncertainty and support better communication outcomes by offering precise instructions and expectations.

Another necessary approach is to use visual aids and social stories to enhance understanding. Visual supports such as pictures, diagrams, or charts can assist individuals with PDAs in comprehending abstract concepts or social situations. Social stories, which describe social interactions in a structured and predictable manner, can also be beneficial in preparing individuals with PDAs for various social scenarios.

Empathy training is a valuable tool in addressing social communication barriers for individuals with PDA. Caregivers can help individuals with PDA develop empathy by teaching them to recognize emotions in themselves and others, understand different perspectives and respond empathetically in social situations. Building empathy skills can enhance social relationships and improve communication dynamics.

Role-playing exercises can effectively practice social skills and increase confidence in social interactions. By engaging individuals with PDA in role-playing scenarios that mimic real-life situations, caregivers can provide opportunities for them to practice appropriate responses, verbal cues, and body language cues in a safe and supportive environment.

Establishing routines and structure in social interactions can also benefit individuals with PDAs. Predictability and consistency can reduce anxiety and create a sense of security during social exchanges. By establishing clear routines for social events or engagements, caregivers can help individuals with PDAs feel more comfortable and prepared for interactions.

Understanding the nuanced needs of individuals with PDA is essential for their support and development. By recognizing how extreme anxiety manifests in behaviors such as avoidance, manipulation, and control mechanisms, caregivers and professionals are better equipped to provide appropriate interventions. These behaviors are not choices but survival strategies individuals employ to cope with overwhelming demands.

The challenges associated with sensory processing difficulties and emotional regulation can profoundly impact daily functioning. Adequate support requires tailored strategies that accommodate these sensory preferences and help individuals manage their emotions more effectively. Practical measures, such as creating predictable environments and clear, concise communication, can significantly reduce anxiety levels.

Moreover, addressing social communication barriers is crucial. By implementing strategies that enhance understanding and interaction, such as explicit teaching of social rules or visual aids, individuals with PDA can experience improved social engagement. This proactive approach fosters a sense of inclusion and community belonging.

It's essential for everyone involved—family, educators, therapists—to adopt a compassionate understanding of these unique challenges. Empathy combined with actionable strategies can make a substantial difference in managing PDA effectively. Encouraging self-awareness and self-regulation skills empowers individuals with PDA, helping them navigate their world with increased confidence and less anxiety.

You can create supportive environments that promote growth and learning by embracing these insights and approaches. Remember, small changes in approach can significantly improve the well-being of individuals with PDA. Actively engage with these strategies to see tangible results in managing anxieties and navigating demands more successfully.

Chapter 3: Tailoring Strategies: Crafting an Individualized Support Plan

"Difference is of the essence of humanity."

John Hume

Unveiling the Art of Individualized Support in PDA

Pathological Demand Avoidance (PDA) presents a complex challenge in behavioral support, requiring a nuanced understanding and approach that diverges significantly from traditional methods. The core of effectively supporting individuals with PDAs lies in recognizing the condition and meticulously crafting support plans that address the unique dimensions of each individual's needs. This understanding forms the foundation of our discussion on developing individualized strategies that align with the preferences and challenges faced by those with PDAs.

At the heart of this approach is acknowledging diverse methodologies in supporting individuals with this condition. Traditional behavioral interventions often fall short, as they do not account for the intense anxiety and need for control experienced by individuals with PDA. Instead, a blend of low-demand strategies and empowerment through choice has shown promising results. These strategies prioritize reducing demands while simultaneously providing individuals with options, thereby reducing anxiety and enhancing engagement.

The effectiveness of any intervention hinges on its ability to resonate with the individual it aims to support. For individuals with PDA, interventions must be more than adaptable—they must be deeply personalized. This involves understanding each person's specific anxieties, triggers, and preferences. Cognitive-behavioral strategies tailored to challenge avoidance behaviors gently and incrementally introduce demands can be particularly beneficial when combined with therapies addressing sensory sensitivities.

Step-by-Step Process: "Pathway to Personalization"

Step 1: Review different approaches to supporting individuals with PDA

Understanding begins with a comprehensive review of available strategies. Low-demand techniques focus on minimizing direct commands and instead offer choices that empower the individual. This flexibility can significantly lessen resistance and anxiety, creating a more conducive environment for cooperation and learning.

Step 2: Discover tailored interventions for PDA's complex needs

Each individual's response to PDA is unique, necessitating tailored interventions. Techniques such as graduated exposure help manage demand-related anxiety gradually and effectively. Additionally, integrating sensory integration therapy can address underlying sensory processing challenges often accompanying PDA, further easing stress and improving overall responsiveness.

Step 3: Learn to develop a customizable support plan

Creating an effective support plan starts with an in-depth understanding of an individual's specific needs and preferences. This plan should outline clear, attainable goals and detail strategic approaches adapted to various settings such as home, school, or community environments. Regular reviews and adaptations of this plan ensure it remains relevant and effective over time.

This structured approach facilitates a better understanding among caregivers and educators about what works best for individuals with PDAs and empowers them to implement these strategies confidently. Focusing on personalization rather than a one-size-fits-all strategy makes support more meaningful and effective, leading to better outcomes for those with PDAs.

Through this detailed exploration, readers will gain insights into effectively navigating the complexities of PDA support, armed with practical tools and strategies that honor these unique individuals' challenges and strengths. The journey towards mastering these tailored approaches promises improved daily interactions and fosters a deeper connection and understanding between individuals with PDAs and those who support them.

Supporting individuals with Pathological Demand Avoidance (PDA) requires a tailored approach considering each person's unique needs and preferences. There are various schools of thought regarding providing support, ranging from low-demand strategies to empowering individuals through choices. Low-demand strategies focus on reducing demands and expectations placed on the individual, creating a more relaxed environment where they can feel less overwhelmed. On the other hand, empowerment through choices emphasizes offering individuals with PDA a sense of control and autonomy in decision-making, which can help build confidence and reduce anxiety.

Understanding the individual: One key aspect of crafting an individualized support plan for someone with PDA is understanding the individual's specific triggers, preferences, and challenges. Each person with a PDA is unique, and what works for one individual may not work for another. Observing and listening to the person can provide valuable insights into what strategies may be most effective in supporting them.

Balancing demands: Striking a balance between reducing demands and empowering choices is crucial in supporting individuals with PDAs. While reducing demands can help alleviate stress and anxiety, offering choices can enable individuals to feel more in control of their environment. Finding the right balance between these two approaches is critical to creating a support plan that resonates with the individual's needs.

Flexibility in strategies: It's essential to remain flexible in implementing strategies for individuals with PDAs. What works one day may not work the next, so being adaptable and willing to adjust support strategies based on the individual's needs is essential. Flexibility allows for a more responsive and effective support system that can evolve with the individual's changing requirements.

Collaboration and communication: Working collaboratively with individuals with PDAs, their families, and caregivers is vital in developing an effective support plan. Open communication and feedback loops can help ensure the support meets the individual's needs and positively impacts their well-being. A more holistic and comprehensive approach to support can be achieved by involving all stakeholders in the process.

Empowering through understanding: Empowering individuals with PDA involves fostering an environment of learning, acceptance, and respect. Acknowledging their unique challenges and strengths can create a supportive atmosphere that encouraging growth and self-confidence. Empathy plays a significant role in building trust and rapport with individuals with PDA, paving the way for more effective support interventions.

Crafting Tailored Interventions for Individuals with Pathological Demand Avoidance (PDA)

Tailored interventions are essential in effectively addressing the complex needs of individuals with PDAs. Understanding the unique characteristics and challenges that come with PDA is crucial in developing personalized strategies that resonate with each individual's specific requirements. By tailoring interventions, we can create effective support plans that respect the individual's autonomy and preferences.

One key aspect of tailored interventions is to recognize the triggers and stressors that can lead to meltdowns or challenging behaviors in individuals with PDA. By identifying these triggers, caregivers and support providers can work on proactive strategies to prevent escalation. Empathy plays a significant role here, as understanding the individual's perspective can aid in creating environments that are conducive to their well-being.

Another essential element of tailored interventions is fostering a sense of predictability and routine. Individuals with PDA often struggle with uncertainty and transitions, which can trigger anxiety and distress. Establishing clear routines and providing advance notice of any changes can help alleviate some of these challenges.

Individualized support plans should also focus on building trust and rapport with the individual. Trust is foundational in any relationship, but it holds particular significance for individuals with PDA, who may have experienced past misunderstandings or struggles in social interactions. By nurturing trust, caregivers can create a safe space where individuals feel understood and supported.

Communication strategies play a vital role in tailored interventions for individuals with PDA. Clear, concise language, avoiding ambiguous statements, and providing visual support can enhance communication effectiveness. Active listening is equally important; it demonstrates respect for the individual's thoughts and feelings while promoting a collaborative approach to problem-solving.

Sensory sensitivities are common among individuals with PDA, so incorporating sensory regulation techniques into tailored interventions can be highly beneficial. Creating sensory-friendly environments, offering sensory tools for self-regulation, and allowing breaks when needed are all strategies to help individuals manage sensory overload effectively.

Collaboration among caregivers, educators, therapists, and other support providers is essential in developing comprehensive, tailored interventions for individuals with PDAs. Each member brings unique insights and expertise, contributing to a holistic approach that addresses the individual's needs from various angles.

Tailoring an Individualized Support Plan for PDA

The Strategic Support Framework for PDA is a comprehensive guide designed to assist caregivers, educators, and therapists in creating personalized plans that cater to the unique needs of individuals with Pathological Demand Avoidance (PDA). The framework comprises several vital steps that work synergistically to ensure the individual's well-being and growth.

Identifying Strengths and Interests

The first step in the framework involves recognizing and leveraging the individual's strengths and interests. This initial phase is crucial as it establishes trust-building and engagement. By acknowledging what the individual excels at and enjoys, caregivers can establish a positive rapport that forms the basis for further interventions.

Comprehensive Assessment

Following the identification of strengths, a thorough assessment process ensues. This stage encompasses observing behaviors across various settings, soliciting feedback from involved parties such as family members or teachers, and understanding the individual's sensory preferences and triggers. A holistic assessment ensures that interventions are tailored to address specific needs effectively.

Collaborative Goal Setting

Once strengths and needs are identified through assessment, collaborative goal setting comes into play. Goals should be meaningful, achievable, and co-created with the individual. Involving them in this process instills a sense of ownership, motivating active participation in their support plan.

Intervention Planning

With goals established, intervention planning can begin. This phase integrates the individual's strengths into strategies while incorporating low-demand approaches to minimize stress. Additionally, indirect communication techniques like declarative language can enhance understanding and cooperation.

Flexible Implementation

The successful implementation of the support plan relies on flexibility. Regular monitoring allows for adjustments based on the individual's response to interventions. Flexibility ensures that strategies can be modified to suit changing needs or circumstances, fostering continuous progress.

Evaluation and Reflection

Evaluation and reflection are essential components of the framework to measure progress accurately. Assessing advancement towards set goals prioritizes the individual's well-being as the ultimate measure of success. Reflecting on outcomes enables the refinement of strategies for future support.

Emphasis on Autonomy and Relationships

Throughout the framework, emphasis is placed on fostering autonomy, enhancing self-regulation skills, and nurturing positive relationships. These elements form the cornerstone of adequate support for individuals with PDA, promoting independence and emotional well-being.

Integrating case examples into the framework illustrates its practical application in real-world scenarios, by providing tangible instances of how each step can be implemented, caregivers and professionals better understand how to tailor support plans effectively for individuals with PDAs.

Crafting an individualized support plan for those with Pathological Demand Avoidance (PDA) is beneficial and essential. The diversity in approaches, from low-demand strategies to empowering through choices, highlights a fundamental truth: one size does not fit all. This chapter has underscored the importance of effectively personalizing intervention strategies to meet each individual's unique needs and preferences.

Understanding the complex needs of someone with PDA requires a compassionate approach, where the primary focus is on fostering a supportive environment that encourages growth and autonomy. By integrating tailored interventions, we address their immediate challenges and empower them to manage their condition proactively. The goal is clear: to enhance their quality of life through strategies that they find manageable and supportive.

To successfully implement these personalized support plans, involving individuals with PDAs in the planning process is crucial. This inclusion ensures that the strategies resonate with them and are more likely to be effective. Remember, empowerment comes from making informed choices, and when individuals feel in control, they are more engaged in managing their challenges.

Take action today. Begin by observing and understanding the specific preferences and triggers of the individual. Use this knowledge to adapt your approach—adjusting demands or increasing choice flexibility. The effectiveness of your support will grow significantly when it aligns closely with their personal experiences and needs.

Finally, remember that you are not alone in this journey. Many have successfully navigated these challenges and found pathways that lead to remarkable improvements in daily living and overall well-being. By applying these personalized strategies, you take a significant step toward transforming challenges into opportunities for success and fulfillment.

Let this be your guiding principle: Empower, engage, and tailor support to unlock the full potential of those with PDAs. Your efforts can make a profound difference in their lives, fostering resilience and independence that lasts a lifetime.

Chapter 4: The Language of Support: Using Declarative Language and Choice

"It is not our differences that divide us. It is

our inability to recognize, accept, and

celebrate those differences."

Audre Lorde

Transforming Challenges into Opportunities: Mastering Declarative Language and Choice in PDA

Pathological Demand Avoidance (PDA), a profile on the autism spectrum, presents unique challenges and opportunities in communication and behavior management. For individuals with PDA, traditional methods of instruction and interaction often prove counterproductive, exacerbating anxiety and triggering resistance. However, by strategically using declarative language and offering choices, caregivers and educators can preempt challenging behaviors, reduce stress, and foster a collaborative environment.

Declarative language forms the cornerstone of effective communication with individuals exhibiting PDA traits. Unlike imperative commands that demand action, declarative sentences share information or feelings without expecting a direct response. This subtle shift in communication style can significantly decrease perceived demands, helping individuals with PDA feel less pressured and more in control of their interactions.

For instance, instead of instructing, "Please clean your room now," a declarative approach would be, "I see a lot of clothes on the floor." This informs and invites the individual to process the information at their own pace, often leading to voluntary action without requiring direct commands.

Offering choices is another critical strategy that empowers individuals with PDAs. When people feel they have agency in decision-making, their motivation increases, and anxiety decreases. These choices must be meaningful yet manageable to avoid overwhelming the individual. Structuring options such as, "Would you like to start your homework at 5 PM or 6 PM?" provides a sense of control while subtly reinforcing the expectation of completing homework.

Recognizing early signs of anxiety is equally important to prevent escalation. Common indicators include increased restlessness, avoidance behaviors, or heightened sensory sensitivity. By identifying these signs early, caregivers can employ strategies such as providing a quiet space or engaging in calming activities to address anxiety proactively.

Step-by-Step Guide: Crafting Calm

Step 1: Master the Art of Declarative Language

Begin by understanding and defining declarative language—sharing thoughts or observations without expecting immediate action. Regularly incorporate this style in daily interactions by commenting on what is happening or sharing how a situation makes you feel. This approach reduces pressure and fosters voluntary cooperation from individuals with PDAs.

Step 2: Understand the Power of Choice Offering

Ensure that choices are simple yet empowering. Start by offering two options that lead to the same end goal but provide autonomy in how to reach it. Collaborate with the individual to explore their preferred choices and how they wish to structure their decision-making process.

Step 3: Identify Early Signs of Anxiety and Employ Strategies to Prevent Escalation

Educate yourself on recognizing subtle changes in behavior or mood that may indicate increasing anxiety. Implement calming strategies immediately upon noticing these signs. Create environments that offer safety and reassurance, using declarative language and structured choices to enhance stability.

Each step should be approached thoughtfully and reviewed regularly for effectiveness. Adjustments may be necessary as you learn what resonates best with the individual you're supporting.

This chapter serves as a guide and an invitation to transform everyday challenges into opportunities for growth and understanding. By mastering these approaches, caregivers can significantly improve their ability to support individuals with PDA effectively—encouraging them towards greater autonomy and reduced anxiety in everyday situations.

Mastering the art of declarative language can be a powerful tool in preempting challenging behaviors and fostering collaboration with individuals with Pathological Demand Avoidance (PDA). By using clear and direct statements, caregivers and educators can help create a supportive environment that minimizes anxiety triggers and empowers individuals with PDA to manage their emotions effectively. Declarative language involves making statements or observations rather than asking questions or giving commands, which can be particularly beneficial for those with PDA who may struggle with demands or requests.

When communicating with someone with a PDA, it is essential to provide choices whenever possible. Giving choices empowers individuals by giving them a sense of control and helps reduce anxiety by avoiding situations where they feel overwhelmed by external demands. Presenting options rather than directives allows individuals to decide based on their preferences and comfort levels. This approach can lead to more positive interactions and decrease the likelihood of resistance or meltdowns.

Recognizing early signs of anxiety is crucial in preventing challenging behaviors in individuals with PDA. By being attuned to subtle cues such as increased restlessness, repetitive behaviors, or verbal cues indicating distress, caregivers, and educators can intervene proactively to de-escalate the situation before it escalates. Employing strategies such as offering sensory tools, providing quiet spaces for relaxation, or engaging in calming activities can help individuals regulate their emotions and prevent meltdowns.

Empathy and understanding are critical components in supporting individuals with PDA. By acknowledging their unique challenges and approaching interactions with compassion and patience, caregivers and educators can build trust and rapport, creating a safe space for communication and collaboration. Validation of their feelings and experiences can help individuals feel heard and respected, fostering a positive environment where they feel supported and understood.

Empowering Through Choices: Supporting Individuals with Pathological Demand Avoidance (PDA)

Giving choices is a powerful tool for supporting individuals with Pathological Demand Avoidance (PDA). By providing options, you empower them to make decisions and take control of their environment, which can help reduce anxiety and prevent challenging behaviors. Choice is a fundamental aspect of autonomy and independence, crucial for individuals with PDA who often struggle with feeling overwhelmed by external demands. They can feel more in charge of their actions and surroundings when presented with choices, leading to increased cooperation and decreased resistance.

Empowering individuals with PDA through choices involves understanding their preferences and limitations. By offering alternatives in tasks or activities, you acknowledge their need for control and respect their unique way of processing information. This approach fosters a sense of agency and promotes self-regulation and emotional well-being. Choices act as a buffer against anxiety triggers, allowing individuals with PDA to navigate situations more comfortably and confidently.

When implementing choice-based strategies, it is essential to be mindful of the options provided. Offering realistic choices that align with the individual's capabilities can enhance their sense of competence and reduce feeling overwhelmed. You create a supportive environment that encourages participation and engagement by tailoring choices to their interests and strengths. Personalizing the options demonstrates understanding and empathy, establishing a positive dynamic built on collaboration and mutual respect.

Incorporating choices into daily interactions can be transformative for individuals with PDAs. Giving them a say in big and small decisions promotes self-advocacy and builds essential life skills. This practice not only empowers them but also strengthens their ability to manage anxiety-provoking situations effectively. Choices serve as a roadmap for navigating challenges, offering a sense of direction amidst uncertainty and instilling confidence in decision-making abilities.

Recognizing the significance of choices in supporting individuals with PDA is critical to fostering a harmonious environment where they can thrive. Empowerment through decision-making cultivates self-esteem and resilience, enabling them to confront obstacles with courage and determination. By embracing the power of choices, you pave the way for collaborative relationships built on trust and understanding. Each option presented is an opportunity for growth and empowerment, laying the groundwork for effective communication and positive outcomes in managing PDA-related challenges.

Identifying early signs of anxiety in individuals with Pathological Demand Avoidance (PDA) is crucial for preventing escalation and challenging behaviors. By recognizing these signs, caregivers, and supporters can intervene early, offering strategies to manage anxiety effectively. Observing changes in behavior, such as increased restlessness, fidgeting, or avoidance of specific tasks, can signal rising anxiety levels. Individuals with PDA may also exhibit verbal clues like repetitive questioning, seeking reassurance, or expressing a need for control as anxiety mounts.

Creating a supportive environment that acknowledges and responds to these early signs is essential to prevent escalation. Implementing calming techniques, such as deep breathing exercises and sensory tools, or providing a safe space for the individual to retreat to when feeling overwhelmed can help regulate emotions before they intensify. Establishing a predictable routine and clear expectations can also reduce uncertainty and anxiety triggers.

Open communication plays a vital role in identifying and addressing anxiety in individuals with PDA. Encouraging them to express their emotions without judgment fosters trust and allows for early intervention when anxiety starts to build. Using declarative language can help convey understanding and support without adding pressure or demands that may exacerbate anxiety levels. By offering choices and empowering individuals with PDAs to make decisions about their environment and activities, supporters can provide a sense of control that can alleviate anxiety.

Strategies such as visual schedules, social stories, or incorporating special interests into daily routines can also be preventive measures against escalating anxiety. These tools offer predictability and structure while catering to the individual's preferences and strengths. Recognizing patterns in behavior can aid in identifying triggers for anxiety, enabling supporters to address potential stressors before they lead to challenging behaviors proactively.

By being proactive in identifying early signs of anxiety and employing strategies to prevent escalation, caregivers and supporters can create a nurturing environment that promotes emotional well-being for individuals with PDA. Empowering them with tools and support to manage their anxiety effectively not only enhances their quality of life but also fosters independence and self-regulation skills. Through consistent observation, communication, and intervention, individuals with PDAs can learn to navigate their emotions successfully and thrive in supportive environments tailored to their unique needs.

In mastering the art of declarative language, we pave the way for preempting challenging behaviors and fostering a spirit of collaboration. This approach not only simplifies communication but also enhances mutual understanding and respect. By shifting from directive to declarative statements, we invite cooperation rather than demand compliance, creating a more harmonious interaction that respects the unique needs of individuals with PDAs.

Offering choices is equally transformative. It empowers individuals by giving them control over their environment, crucial in mitigating anxiety. When people feel they have agency, their stress levels decrease, and they are more likely to engage positively. This empowerment is a simple yet profound tool that can significantly alter the dynamics of any interaction.

Recognizing early signs of anxiety is another critical skill that can prevent many challenging situations from escalating. Early intervention strategies are essential in maintaining calm and ensuring that individuals are not overwhelmed by their circumstances. Implementing these strategies effectively requires vigilance and an empathetic understanding of the subtle cues that indicate distress.

Implement these practices consistently to see a noticeable improvement in interactions and overall well-being. These methods involve managing behaviors and nurturing an environment where everyone can thrive. Your proactive efforts in applying these techniques will foster a supportive atmosphere that encouraging growth and development.

Remember, every step you take towards using a declarative language, offering choices, and identifying early signs of anxiety not only helps in immediate situations but also builds long-term skills for managing PDA effectively. Engage with these strategies actively; they are powerful tools in your journey toward understanding and supporting unique minds.

By embracing these approaches, you affirm your commitment to creating a supportive and empowering environment. This commitment is your pathway to fostering lasting change and helping individuals with PDA navigate their world confidently and efficiently.

Chapter 5: Sensory-Friendly Environments and Self-Regulation

"Do not fear to be eccentric in opinion, for

every opinion now accepted

was once eccentric."

Bertrand Russell

Harnessing Harmony: Crafting Calm Spaces for Unique Minds

Pathological Demand Avoidance (PDA), a complex and often misunderstood profile within the autism spectrum, presents unique challenges that extend beyond typical behavioral strategies. Individuals with PDA experience an intense need to control their environment and avoid everyday demands, which sensory sensitivities and difficulties in self-regulation can often exacerbate. Recognizing and addressing these sensory challenges is not just beneficial but crucial in supporting their overall well-being and reducing anxiety.

The core of creating a supportive atmosphere for individuals with PDA involves implementing sensory-friendly strategies. These strategies are designed to mitigate the overwhelming sensory input that can lead to distress or meltdowns. By adjusting the physical environment and daily routines, caregivers and educators can significantly improve the quality of life for those with PDAs.

Moreover, fostering self-regulation skills through techniques such as mindfulness has shown promising results in helping individuals manage their responses to sensory stimuli. This approach not only aids in controlling their reactions but also empowers them with tools to handle stress more effectively. Thus, integrating mindfulness and other self-regulation practices into their routine is a transformative step towards autonomy and emotional resilience.

Creating environments that support well-being goes beyond mere physical adjustments; it involves a holistic understanding of an individual's needs and preferences. This chapter delves into practical ways to establish such environments, ensuring they are both soothing and conducive to personal growth for individuals with PDAs.

Step 1: Implement Sensory-Friendly Strategies

The first step involves tailoring the environment to reduce sensory overload, which is a common trigger for anxiety in individuals with PDA. Techniques include:

- We provide sensory tools like fidget toys or noise-canceling headphones to help manage sensory input.
- We are utilizing visual schedules to reduce uncertainty about daily activities, which can be a source of stress.
- They are creating designated quiet areas where individuals can retreat when overwhelmed.

This phase emphasizes the importance of involving individuals in discussions about their sensory preferences, ensuring that modifications are genuinely beneficial.

Step 2: Utilize Mindfulness and Other Techniques for Self-Regulation

Introducing mindfulness can significantly enhance an individual's ability to regulate emotions and responses to sensory stimuli. Steps include:

- Practicing deep breathing exercises promotes relaxation and focus.
- Conducting body scans to increase body awareness and detect early signs of stress.
- Applying grounding techniques to connect with the present

moment reduces anxiety.

In addition to mindfulness, incorporating physical activities and regular sensory breaks can further aid self-regulation, offering a comprehensive approach to managing sensitivity.

Step 3: Create Supportive Environments for Better Self-Management of Anxiety

The final step focuses on establishing structured yet flexible environments that encourage individuals with PDA to manage their anxiety proactively. Strategies include:

- Ensuring predictability and structure, which provide a sense of security.
- Organizing the physical space in a way that minimizes stress triggers.
- Promoting flexibility within boundaries allows individuals some control over their activities without overwhelming them.

This stage is crucial for fostering an atmosphere where individuals feel safe, supported, and capable of exploring their capacities without undue stress.

By methodically implementing these steps, caregivers and educators can create a nurturing environment that significantly alleviates the challenges faced by those with Pathological Demand Avoidance. Each strategy addresses immediate concerns related to sensory sensitivities and builds long-term skills that empower individuals with PDA to navigate their world more effectively. Through mindful adjustments and compassionate understanding, we can unlock a path to greater autonomy and emotional well-being for those affected by PDA.

Individuals with Pathological Demand Avoidance (PDA) often experience sensory sensitivities that can significantly impact their daily lives. Sensory-friendly strategies play a crucial role in alleviating these sensitivities and creating environments that promote well-being for individuals with PDA. By understanding and implementing sensory-friendly approaches, caregivers and educators can make a positive difference in the lives of those with PDAs.

One effective strategy is to provide a sensory-friendly environment by minimizing sensory triggers. This includes reducing noise levels, controlling lighting, and organizing spaces to avoid overwhelming stimuli. Creating designated quiet areas where individuals can retreat when feeling overwhelmed can also be beneficial. Sensory tools like noise-canceling headphones, fidget toys, or weighted blankets can offer comfort and help regulate sensory input.

Routine and predictability are essential for individuals with PDA. Establishing consistent schedules and clear expectations can help reduce anxiety and provide a sense of control. Offering visual schedules or using timers to signal transitions can aid in preparing individuals for changes in activities or environments.

Encouraging movement breaks throughout the day can help regulate sensory input and provide opportunities for physical release. Simple stretching exercises or short walks can be incorporated into daily routines to support self-regulation.

Another crucial aspect of creating a sensory-friendly environment is respecting individual preferences. Understanding each person's unique sensitivities and preferences allows caregivers and educators to tailor strategies that best meet their needs. By listening to feedback and observing reactions, adjustments can be made to ensure the comfort and well-being of individuals with PDAs.

Cultivating Self-Regulation: Mindfulness and Techniques for Individuals with Pathological Demand Avoidance (PDA)

Implementing mindfulness and other self-regulation techniques can be powerful tools in helping individuals with Pathological Demand Avoidance (PDA) navigate their emotions and responses more effectively. Mindfulness, a practice that involves being present in the moment without judgment, can aid in developing self-awareness and emotional regulation. Encouraging individuals with PDA to engage in mindfulness exercises can help them recognize their sensory triggers and manage their reactions proactively.

One effective technique is deep breathing exercises. By focusing on their breath, individuals with PDA can center themselves during moments of stress or sensory overload. Teaching them to take slow, deep breaths can activate the body's relaxation response, reducing anxiety levels and promoting a sense of calm. These exercises can be practiced regularly to build resilience and enhance self-regulation skills over time.

Another beneficial strategy is progressive muscle relaxation. This technique involves tensing and then relaxing different muscle groups in the body, helping to release physical tension and promote relaxation. Individuals with PDA can learn to identify areas of tension during stressful moments and use this technique to release built-up stress, fostering a sense of control over their physical responses.

Visual imagery techniques can also aid in self-regulation. Encouraging individuals with PDA to visualize peaceful scenes or positive outcomes can shift their focus from stressors to calming mental images. This practice can help reduce anxiety and promote well-being by positively engaging the imagination.

Creating sensory toolkits tailored to individual preferences can enhance self-regulation skills. These toolkits may include fidget toys, noise-canceling headphones, or textured objects that individuals with PDAs find soothing. Access to these tools allows them to regulate their sensory experiences in challenging environments, empowering them to manage overwhelming stimuli effectively.

Encouraging regular physical activity can also support self-regulation. Activities like yoga, dance, or nature walks can help individuals with PDA release pent-up energy and tension, promoting emotional balance and self-control. Physical exercise has been shown to reduce anxiety levels and improve overall well-being, making it a valuable component of a self-regulation routine.

Promoting consistent routines and schedules is essential for fostering self-regulation skills in individuals with PDA. Establishing predictable daily routines helps create a sense of stability and security, reducing anxiety levels and providing a framework for managing tasks and transitions effectively. By following a structured schedule, individuals with PDA can anticipate upcoming events and prepare themselves mentally, leading to smoother transitions and reduced stress levels.

Incorporating these mindfulness techniques, sensory toolkits, physical activities, and structured routines into daily life can empower individuals with PDAs to enhance their self-regulation skills and navigate challenging situations more effectively. By consistently supporting and guiding in practicing these strategies, caregivers, and educators can help individuals with PDA build resilience, manage anxiety, and cultivate emotional well-being in their daily lives.

Sensory Integration and Self-Regulation Framework

The assessment phase is the first crucial step in the Sensory Integration and Self-Regulation Framework. This initial stage involves identifying the individual's sensory preferences and aversions and recognizing triggers that may lead to overwhelm or distress. Understanding these elements is fundamental in customizing environments to minimize sensory overloads and create a more supportive setting for individuals with PDAs.

Moving on to the customization step, adjustments are made to both home and educational settings to reduce potential stressors. This may involve simple modifications like adjusting lighting, reducing background noise, or introducing sensory aids like weighted blankets. By tailoring the environment to suit the individual's sensory needs, it becomes a place where they can feel more comfortable and secure.

The framework also emphasizes teaching self-regulation techniques as a critical component in managing anxiety. Techniques like mindfulness exercises, deep breathing, and visual schedules play a significant role in helping individuals with PDA regulate their emotions and responses to sensory stimuli. By providing them with these tools, they can learn to navigate challenging situations more effectively.

Collaboration is a central theme throughout the framework. Involving the individual with PDA in the adaptation process empowers them to have a say in the changes made to their environment and the strategies taught to them. This collaborative approach fosters a sense of autonomy and ensures that interventions are tailored to their specific needs and preferences.

Practical examples of successful adaptations within this framework serve as actionable guidance for caregivers and educators. By implementing these strategies, individuals with PDA can experience calmer environments that support their overall well-being and enhance their ability to manage anxiety effectively.

The Sensory Integration and Self-Regulation Framework provides a systematic approach to creating supportive environments for individuals with PDA. By assessing sensory needs, customizing environments, teaching self-regulation techniques, and fostering collaboration, caregivers and educators can empower individuals with PDAs to thrive in their surroundings.

Understanding and addressing the sensory needs of individuals with PDA (Pathological Demand Avoidance) is beneficial and crucial. By implementing sensory-friendly strategies, we can significantly alleviate the discomfort caused by sensory sensitivities. This proactive approach enables these individuals to engage more fully in their environments, reducing anxiety and enhancing overall well-being.

Incorporating mindfulness and other self-regulation techniques offers another layer of support, empowering those with PDA to manage their reactions and emotions more effectively. These skills are essential, as they foster a sense of control and resilience, allowing individuals to navigate daily challenges more easily.

Creating supportive environments goes beyond physical adjustments; it involves a holistic understanding of what makes an environment truly nurturing for someone with PDA. This includes everything from the physical setting to the emotional climate, all tailored to encourage autonomy and minimize stress triggers.

The synergy of these strategies—sensory adjustment, mindful practice, and supportive environmental structuring—creates a foundation for success. It is a proactive formula that addresses immediate needs and builds long-term resilience and adaptability.

Each step taken towards this integrated approach is a step towards enabling individuals with PDAs to lead more fulfilling lives. The benefits extend beyond individuals, positively impacting families, educators, and caregivers. It's about creating a compassionate framework that acknowledges unique needs while fostering an atmosphere where everyone can thrive.

By embracing these strategies, you are not just responding to challenges—you anticipate and mitigate them, transforming potential obstacles into opportunities for growth and development. Engage actively with these approaches; the results will be rewarding and profoundly transformative.

Chapter 6: Unveiling PDA: From Misunderstanding to Mastery

"A flower does not think of competing

with the flower next to it.

It just blooms."

Zen Shin

Peeling Back the Layers of PDA

Pathological Demand Avoidance (PDA) is a complex and often misunderstood profile associated with autism that poses unique challenges to those it affects and their support networks. By understanding the nuances of PDA behaviors, we can foster empathy and tailor support to meet individual needs effectively. This chapter aims to unravel the intricacies of PDA, providing practical strategies to aid individuals in various settings, from educational environments to everyday interactions.

At its core, PDA involves an intense avoidance of everyday demands and expectations, which can manifest as extreme stress, anxiety, and behaviors that are often perceived as socially inappropriate. These actions are not willful or manipulative but are coping mechanisms for overwhelming demands. Recognizing this can significantly shift our perspective and approach, moving from judgment to support.

The first key takeaway is the demystification of PDA behaviors. Understanding that these behaviors are responses to feeling out of control or overload is vital. Simplifying our understanding doesn't just benefit caregivers and educators—it empowers them to approach situations with a new level of insight and compassion.

Secondly, the chapter provides practical strategies and interventions. These are designed to be straightforward and actionable, ensuring they can be implemented across different scenarios. From adjusting communication methods to modifying environmental factors, these strategies aim to reduce demand sensitivity and increase engagement and cooperation from individuals with PDAs.

Moreover, equipping readers with practical tools is a cornerstone of this discussion. These tools do not require extensive training or significant lifestyle changes; they involve minor adjustments that make substantial differences. Techniques such as offering choices instead of commands or using indirect language can transform interactions and outcomes.

Understanding leads to better support systems. By embracing a compassionate approach, stakeholders can create environments where individuals with PDA feel understood rather than pressured. This supportive atmosphere alleviates stress, promotes positive relationships, and enhances the quality of life for everyone involved.

The journey from misunderstanding to mastery involves continuous learning and adjustment. Each individual with a PDA is unique, requiring personalized strategies that respect their specific needs and boundaries. This chapter encourages an ongoing commitment to learning—a dynamic process where each step taken improves understanding and support.

In essence, mastering PDA support is not about overcoming a challenge but transforming our approach to engagement and care. Through knowledge, empathy, and practical action, we empower ourselves and others to foster environments where individuals with PDA can thrive. This transformation in approach is not just beneficial—it's necessary for creating inclusive communities that honor every individual's potential.

Navigating the world of Pathological Demand Avoidance (PDA) can be overwhelming and confusing for those unfamiliar with this complex condition. Demystifying PDA behaviors is the first step towards fostering understanding and empathy for individuals grappling with this neurological difference. By unraveling the intricacies of PDA, we can begin to see beyond the surface-level behaviors and delve into the underlying causes and needs of those affected.

PDA behaviors, often misunderstood as mere defiance or stubbornness, are, in fact, intricate coping mechanisms that individuals with PDA employ to manage overwhelming anxiety and sensory issues. By reframing these behaviors as adaptive responses rather than intentional defiance, we can shift our perspective toward empathy and support. Recognizing that these behaviors stem from a place of distress rather than disobedience is crucial in developing effective strategies to help individuals with PDA thrive.

Acknowledging that PDA behaviors are not a choice but a manifestation of internal struggles and challenges is essential. Refraining from labeling these behaviors as deliberate acts of disobedience can create a more compassionate and understanding environment for individuals with PDAs. Embracing empathy as a guiding principle allows us to approach these behaviors with patience and kindness, laying the groundwork for meaningful connections and support.

Understanding the underlying motivations behind PDA behaviors opens the door to tailored interventions and strategies that address the unique needs of individuals with PDAs. By peeling back the layers of misunderstanding and misconceptions surrounding PDAs, we pave the way for effective support systems that cater to the specific requirements of those navigating this complex condition. Through education and awareness, we can bridge the gap between misconception and truth, fostering environments where individuals with PDA feel understood and supported.

Tailoring Support Strategies for Individuals with Pathological Demand Avoidance (PDA)

In supporting individuals with PDAs across various settings, it is essential to tailor strategies to meet their unique needs. One practical approach is establishing clear routines and expectations providing a structured environment to help individuals with PDA navigate daily challenges. Consistency is critical; maintaining a predictable schedule can reduce anxiety and enhance feelings of security for individuals with PDAs.

Another valuable strategy is to offer choices within limits. By presenting options while setting clear boundaries, you empower individuals with PDAs to feel a sense of control over their environment without becoming overwhelmed by too many decisions. This approach fosters independence and autonomy while also providing necessary guidance.

Visual supports are potent tools for communication and understanding for individuals with PDAs. Utilizing visual schedules, task lists, or social stories can assist in clarifying expectations and promoting successful interactions. Visual aids help to reduce ambiguity, offering concrete references for individuals with PDAs to follow.

Flexibility and patience are paramount when supporting individuals with PDAs. Understanding that unexpected changes or transitions may trigger distress allows for a more compassionate response. Offering reassurance and allowing time for adjustment can help ease transitions and mitigate potential meltdowns.

Creating a calm, sensory-friendly environment is crucial for individuals with PDAs. Minimizing sensory triggers such as loud noises, bright lights, or crowded spaces can significantly reduce stress levels. Providing sensory tools like fidget toys or noise-canceling headphones offers coping mechanisms for individuals with PDA to regulate their sensory experiences effectively.

Collaboration with professionals and educators is essential in developing tailored support plans for individuals with PDAs. Working closely with therapists, teachers, and other specialists can ensure a holistic approach to addressing the needs of individuals with PDAs across different settings. Regular communication and sharing of strategies can promote consistency in support, enhancing the individual's overall well-being.

Encouraging self-regulation skills through mindfulness techniques and emotional regulation strategies can empower individuals with PDA to manage their emotions effectively. Teaching coping mechanisms like deep breathing exercises or progressive muscle relaxation techniques equips them with valuable tools for navigating challenging situations.

Celebrating successes, no matter how small, is vital in reinforcing positive behaviors and building self-esteem in individuals with PDA. Recognizing efforts and achievements helps foster a sense of accomplishment and motivation to continue growing and developing new skills. Positive reinforcement plays a significant role in shaping behavior and encouraging desired outcomes in various contexts.

By implementing these practical strategies and interventions tailored to the unique needs of individuals with PDA, caregivers, educators, and support providers can create supportive environments that nurture growth and well-being. Through consistency, flexibility, clear communication, and collaboration, it is possible to empower individuals with PDA to thrive across different settings while fostering understanding and acceptance within their communities.

Equipping yourself with the knowledge and tools to transform your approach to PDA is crucial in providing adequate support to individuals with PDAs. Understanding PDA's unique characteristics and challenges is the first step towards creating a supportive environment. Recognizing individuals' specific needs and triggers with PDA allows you to tailor interventions and strategies to meet their requirements effectively.

Adopting a proactive mindset is one key aspect of transforming your approach to PDA. Instead of reacting to challenging behaviors, anticipate triggers and implement preemptive strategies to prevent escalation. Creating structured routines and clear expectations can help individuals with PDA navigate daily tasks more effectively.

Communication plays a vital role in supporting individuals with PDAs. Using clear, concise language and visual supports can enhance understanding and reduce anxiety. Providing choices within boundaries allows individuals with PDAs to feel a sense of control, promoting cooperation and reducing resistance.

Establishing a safe and predictable environment is essential for individuals with PDAs. Minimizing sensory overload by creating quiet spaces or using sensory tools can help regulate emotions and prevent meltdowns. Encouraging self-regulation techniques such as deep breathing exercises or mindfulness practices can empower individuals with PDA to manage their emotions more effectively.

Collaborating with educators, therapists, and other professionals can provide additional support and resources for individuals with PDAs. By sharing information and strategies across different settings, you can create a cohesive support network that promotes consistency and understanding.

Regularly evaluating and adjusting your approach based on individual needs and progress is critical to fostering growth and development in individuals with PDA. Flexibility and patience are essential when supporting individuals with PDA, as progress may be gradual but significant.

By equipping yourself with knowledge, empathy, and practical strategies, you can create a supportive environment where individuals with PDA can thrive. Your commitment to understanding their unique needs and challenges will benefit them and enrich your perspective on neurodiversity and human interaction.

Understanding and supporting individuals with Pathological Demand Avoidance (PDA) requires empathy, knowledge, and practical strategies. This chapter has endeavored to provide a solid foundation in all three areas, emphasizing the importance of seeing beyond surface behaviors to the underlying needs.

Demystifying PDA behaviors is not just about recognizing what these behaviors are but also understanding why they occur. This insight fosters empathy and patience, crucial traits for anyone supporting individuals with PDA. When approaching PDA with understanding rather than judgment, we pave the way for more effective support and healthier relationships.

The practical strategies and interventions discussed here are designed to be applied across various settings, from educational environments to home life. These tools are not merely theoretical but are actionable steps that can lead to significant improvements in managing daily challenges. By adapting these strategies to fit individual needs, caregivers and professionals can offer meaningful and empowering support.

Equipping you with this knowledge aims to transform your approach to PDA, making it more informed and proactive. Knowledge is power, particularly in scenarios where traditional methods fall short. With the right tools, you can make a tangible difference in the lives of those with PDAs.

Moving forward, embrace these insights and strategies with confidence. You can create positive change and foster environments where individuals with PDA can thrive. Remember, every step you take is progress, and continuous learning and adaptation are vital components of mastery in any field.

Let this knowledge empower you not only to support but also to advocate for those with PDAs. Their unique minds offer incredible insights into resilience, creativity, and the diversity of human cognition. By applying what you've learned, you're aiding their daily lives and recognizing and celebrating their unique contributions to our world.

Take action today, armed with new understandings and practical solutions that can bring about real change. Each interaction is an opportunity to apply what you have learned, ensuring that individuals with PDAs receive the understanding and support they deserve.

Chapter 7: Voices of PDA: How Does PDA Manifest in Real Life?

"The only disability in life is a bad attitude."

Scott Hamilton

Unmasking the Everyday: Insights into PDA

Pathological Demand Avoidance (PDA) is a complex behavioral profile that often remains misunderstood yet profoundly impacts the lives of those it touches. This chapter delves deep into the real-life manifestations of PDA, providing a more transparent lens through which family members, educators, and professionals can view and understand these behaviors. The goal is to foster a more empathetic and practical approach to supporting individuals with PDAs by illustrating how it can present in various everyday situations.

PDA is characterized by an extreme avoidance of everyday demands and expectations, which can be misinterpreted as defiance or stubbornness. However, it's crucial to recognize this behavior as part of a broader anxiety-driven need to control situations. Readers can gain a practical understanding of these challenges by exploring situational examples—from how a child with PDA might react to routine school assignments to how adults manage workplace expectations.

These real-life scenarios illuminate the nuanced ways PDAs can manifest and highlight successful strategies for managing these behaviors. For instance, modifying communication styles or adjusting environmental factors can lead to significantly better outcomes. Such adjustments help in reducing the perceived demands and thereby lower anxiety levels in individuals with PDA.

Moreover, this chapter aims to deepen the reader's connection with the subject by outlining effective, personalized strategies that cater to the needs of those with PDAs. It's about moving beyond a one-size-fits-all approach in educational and therapeutic settings to embrace more tailored interventions. These strategies are theoretical and

For families and caregivers, understanding PDA's manifestations goes beyond mere academic interest—it's about building more robust, more supportive relationships that empower individuals with PDA. Implementing simple changes at home, such as offering choices instead of direct demands, can make a substantial difference in daily interactions. Such approaches underscore the importance of flexibility and patience in fostering an environment where individuals with PDA can thrive.

Educators and professionals will find this exploration particularly useful as it provides them with tools to recognize when typical strategies may not be effective and adapt their approaches accordingly. This includes creating learning environments that minimize triggers of demand avoidance and focus on engaging students through their interests.

Ultimately, this chapter serves as a guide for anyone supporting individuals with PDAs. Providing actionable advice backed by real-life examples and success stories encourages readers to take proactive steps toward understanding and meeting the unique needs of those with this profile. The insights here are designed to inform and inspire action and hope in those who may feel overwhelmed by the challenges of PDA.

Through compassionate understanding and targeted support strategies, we can create a world where individuals with Pathological Demand Avoidance are not merely managed but genuinely supported in leading fulfilling lives.

Understanding how Pathological Demand Avoidance (PDA) can manifest in various aspects of daily life is essential for those supporting individuals with this profile. In relationships, families, and educational settings, the behaviors associated with PDA can present unique challenges that require tailored approaches for effective management. For instance, in family dynamics, a child exhibiting PDA traits might resist simple requests like getting ready for school or following a bedtime routine, leading to heightened tension and conflicts within the household. Such situations can be emotionally taxing for both the individual with PDA and their family members, requiring patience and understanding to navigate effectively.

In educational settings, a student with PDA may struggle with transitions between activities, resist following classroom rules, or exhibit meltdowns when faced with demands they perceive as overwhelming. These behaviors can disrupt the learning environment for the entire class and hinder the student's academic progress. Teachers and support staff play a crucial role in recognizing these challenges and implementing strategies to create a supportive and inclusive classroom environment that meets the unique needs of students with PDAs.

Moreover, in social interactions, individuals with PDA may find it challenging to engage in typical conversations or participate in group activities due to their difficulties with social communication and flexibility. This can lead to isolation and frustration, impacting their ability to form meaningful peer connections. Understanding these social dynamics is critical to providing individuals with PDAs the necessary support to navigate social situations successfully.

When managing PDA behaviors in real-life scenarios, adopting a holistic approach that considers the individual's specific triggers and preferences is vital. By acknowledging the underlying anxiety and need for control that often drive PDA behaviors, caregivers, educators, and professionals can develop targeted strategies to help individuals with PDA regulate their emotions and responses effectively. Creating predictable routines, offering choices within limits, and using visual supports are practical techniques that can help reduce anxiety and promote cooperation in daily interactions.

Navigating Real-Life Examples: Strategies for Managing Pathological Demand Avoidance (PDA) Behaviors

Navigating the challenges and successes in managing Pathological Demand Avoidance (PDA) can be complex. Still, by delving into real-life examples of behaviors, we can better understand how to effectively support individuals with this profile. One everyday challenge individuals with PDA face is extreme anxiety when confronted with demands or requests. This can lead to avoidant behaviors such as meltdowns, shutdowns, or verbal aggression. Success in managing these challenges involves recognizing the triggers and tailoring strategies to reduce demands while achieving goals.

Another prevalent behavior seen in individuals with PDA is an apparent lack of compliance or defiance. They may resist instructions, refuse to engage in tasks, or negotiate excessively to avoid demands. Successfully managing this behavior involves offering choices within boundaries, providing clear expectations, and using visual supports to enhance understanding and reduce anxiety surrounding tasks.

Difficulty transitioning between activities is a common struggle for individuals with PDA. Sudden changes or unexpected transitions can lead to heightened anxiety and resistance.

Successfully supporting transitions involves using visual schedules, countdown timers, and providing warnings ahead of changes to help prepare the individual for what's coming next.

Sensory sensitivities are also frequently observed in individuals with PDA, which can exacerbate avoidance behaviors in demanding situations. Effective management of sensory sensitivities includes creating sensory-friendly environments, offering sensory tools for self-regulation, and allowing breaks when sensory input becomes overwhelming.

In instances where individuals with PDA engage in repetitive questioning or seeking reassurance, it's essential to understand that this behavior stems from anxiety and the need for control. Managing this behavior successfully involves providing consistent responses, establishing routines, and offering reassurance within limits to promote a sense of security and predictability.

Moreover, individuals with PDA might exhibit difficulty regulating emotions, leading to intense outbursts or emotional dysregulation when feeling overwhelmed by demands. Supporting emotional regulation includes teaching coping strategies such as deep breathing exercises mindfulness techniques, and creating calming spaces for self-soothing.

In deepening our understanding of Pathological Demand Avoidance (PDA) and its manifestations, we must equip ourselves with effective strategies tailored to the unique needs of individuals with this profile. By implementing targeted approaches, caregivers, educators, and professionals can provide better support and foster successful outcomes in managing PDA behaviors. One key strategy is to offer choices within boundaries to individuals with PDAs, empowering them while maintaining structure and predictability in their environment.

Another crucial aspect is to use clear, concise language when communicating with individuals with PDAs. By avoiding vague instructions or ambiguous requests, clarity can help reduce anxiety and confusion, leading to smoother interactions. Additionally, providing visual supports such as schedules or visual cues can aid in clarifying expectations and transitions for individuals with PDA, promoting a sense of security and predictability.

Consistency plays a significant role in managing PDA behaviors. Establishing consistent routines and boundaries can create a stable environment that reduces uncertainty and stress for individuals with PDA. Moreover, offering praise and positive reinforcement for desired behaviors can motivate individuals with PDA to engage in challenging tasks or activities, fostering a positive learning environment.

Encouraging flexibility is vital when supporting individuals with PDAs. Acknowledging their need for control while gently introducing changes or new experiences can help build their tolerance for unexpected situations. Furthermore, providing opportunities for breaks or downtime can prevent overwhelm and meltdowns, allowing individuals with PDAs to regulate their emotions effectively.

Building trust is a fundamental component of supporting individuals with PDAs. By demonstrating empathy, understanding, and patience, caregivers, educators, and professionals can cultivate strong relationships based on mutual respect and cooperation. By establishing trust, individuals with PDA are more likely to feel safe expressing their needs and concerns, leading to improved communication and collaboration.

In summary, by incorporating strategies such as offering choices within boundaries, using clear communication, providing visual supports, maintaining consistency, offering praise, encouraging flexibility, and building trust, caregivers, educators, and professionals can enhance their support for individuals with PDA. These practical approaches aim to empower individuals with PDA by creating supportive environments that acknowledge their unique strengths and challenges.

Understanding the diverse manifestations of Pathological Demand Avoidance (PDA) in everyday scenarios is crucial. This knowledge is not just academic; it directly enhances the support and strategies we offer to those affected by PDA, enabling them to navigate daily challenges more effectively. Recognizing the signs within varied contexts—from family interactions to educational demands—allows for a more tailored and compassionate approach to intervention.

Everyone with a PDA is unique, and acknowledging this individuality is foundational in developing effective management strategies. The examples discussed here highlight the challenges and triumphs that can come from managing PDA. Success stories are particularly illuminating because they show that positive outcomes are possible with understanding and tailored support.

Practical solutions are paramount. Strategies that seem small can make significant differences, such as adjusting communication styles or rethinking behavior management techniques. These approaches empower caregivers and professionals, offering them tools that are effective and implementable without overwhelming complexity.

Encouraging proactive engagement with these strategies is essential when individuals understand the "why" behind behaviors associated with PDAs. They are better equipped to respond in ways that support self-regulation and cooperation rather than confrontation.

Finally, fostering an environment of emotional mastery and resilience is vital for everyone involved. This chapter aims to reassure you that while the journey might be challenging, you are not alone. There are clear, actionable paths forward that can lead to improved outcomes for individuals with PDA. By embracing these strategies, caregivers and professionals can make a profound difference in the lives of those they support, enhancing daily interactions and long-term development.

Chapter 8: Navigating the Resources Landscape for PDA Support

"Empathy is seeing with the eyes of another, listening

with the ears of another and feeling with

the heart of another."

Alfred Adler

Unlocking Support: Essential Tools and Communities for PDA

Pathological Demand Avoidance (PDA) presents unique challenges and demands a nuanced understanding and approach. This chapter delves into a comprehensive list of resources, diagnostic tools, and community connections designed to empower families, educators, and therapists with the needed knowledge and support. The aim is to equip you with practical tools to simplify managing a PDA and foster an environment of growth and understanding.

Navigating the landscape of support for PDAs involves understanding where and what to look for. An exhaustive list of resources is crucial in providing that first step—guiding you to reliable information, contemporary research, and community experiences. These resources include specialized websites that offer insights into the latest treatments and strategies and connect you to stories from others who are walking a similar path. Online forums serve as a vibrant community space where questions can be posed, experiences shared, and support systems built, thereby reducing the isolation often felt by those dealing with PDA.

Equally important are the tools for diagnosing and assessing PDA. These tools help identify the presence of PDA traits and determine their impact on daily functioning. They range from structured interviews to observation reports explicitly tailored for PDA. Utilizing these tools can help create a more personalized approach to management and intervention, thus enhancing effectiveness. For professionals, these tools provide a framework for assessment rooted in the latest clinical research, ensuring that interventions are evidence-based.

The chapter also emphasizes the importance of connecting with professional organizations and communities. These bodies often offer training sessions, workshops, and seminars that can be invaluable in staying updated with the latest research and effective strategies. For families, joining these organizations can provide a sense of solidarity and access to a wealth of knowledge from professionals who specialize in PDA.

It is essential to recognize that while online resources are invaluable, direct engagement with knowledgeable professionals and communities can significantly enhance understanding and management strategies. These interactions offer real-time support and adjustments to strategies that cater directly to individual needs.

Moreover, this chapter encourages active participation in online and offline PDA networks. Engaging actively with these communities helps gain emotional support and share practical advice that can be adapted to personal circumstances. It's about building a network that supports you just as much as you contribute.

Lastly, navigating these resources should be viewed as an ongoing process rather than a one-time effort. As our understanding of PDA evolves, so too will the resources available. Regular engagement with these tools and communities will ensure that you remain at the forefront of effective strategies for managing PDAs.

By providing these insights into valuable resources, diagnostic tools, and professional communities, this chapter aims to arm you with knowledge—turning challenges into opportunities for growth and empowerment in handling PDAs effectively.

Navigating the resources landscape for PDA support can be daunting, especially when seeking valuable information and connections. In today's digital age, the internet offers many resources, including websites and online forums, that can provide much-needed support, guidance, and understanding for individuals dealing with PDAs and their families.

Online forums can be a lifeline for those feeling isolated or struggling to find people who understand their experiences. Platforms such as Reddit, specialized Facebook groups, and dedicated forums offer a space where individuals can share their stories, seek advice, and connect with others facing similar challenges. These forums often create a sense of community and belonging that can be incredibly comforting for those navigating the complexities of PDA.

Websites dedicated to PDAs can serve as comprehensive repositories of information, resources, and tools for individuals seeking to deepen their understanding of the condition. From articles written by experts to personal accounts from individuals living with PDA, these websites offer a wealth of knowledge that can help demystify the disorder and provide practical tips for managing its challenges effectively.

Diagnostic tools available online can also be instrumental in helping individuals assess whether PDA may be a factor in their lives or the lives of their loved ones. While self-diagnosis is not a substitute for professional assessment, these tools can provide valuable insights and prompt individuals to seek further evaluation from qualified professionals.

In addition to online resources, professional organizations focused on PDA can offer a wealth of information, training opportunities, and networking events for individuals looking to deepen their knowledge and connect with experts in the field. These organizations often host conferences, workshops, and webinars that can be invaluable for professionals working with individuals with PDAs and families seeking support.

Empowering Resources for Diagnosing and Assessing Pathological Demand Avoidance (PDA)

When navigating the landscape of resources for diagnosing and assessing Pathological Demand Avoidance (PDA), having the right tools at your disposal is crucial. Professionals, caregivers, and individuals can benefit significantly from utilizing these resources to understand PDA better and manage its challenges effectively. Here are some practical tools that can aid in the diagnosis and assessment process:

Online Screening Tools

Online screening tools can be a valuable first step in identifying potential signs of PDA. These tools are often designed to provide preliminary assessments based on reported behaviors and symptoms. While they should not replace professional evaluation, they can offer insights that prompt further discussion with healthcare providers or specialists.

Diagnostic Criteria Checklist

A comprehensive checklist based on established diagnostic criteria for PDA can be helpful for individuals seeking self-assessment and professionals conducting evaluations. This checklist typically includes key behavioral characteristics associated with PDA, allowing for a structured approach to identifying potential indicators of the condition.

Behavioral Observation Tools

Behavioral observation tools provide a systematic way to track and document specific behaviors associated with PDA over time. By keeping detailed records of behavior patterns, triggers, and responses, individuals and caregivers can better understand how PDA manifests in daily life. This information can also be valuable for healthcare providers when making diagnoses or treatment recommendations.

Communication Skills Assessment

Assessing communication skills is essential in understanding how individuals with PDA interact with others and express their needs and emotions. Tools that focus on communication styles, social cues interpretation, and emotional regulation can help identify areas of strength and areas that may require additional support or intervention.

Sensory Processing Tools

Sensory processing challenges are common among individuals with PDA, impacting their ability to regulate responses to sensory stimuli. Using sensory processing tools to assess sensory sensitivities, preferences, and coping strategies can provide valuable insights into how sensory issues contribute to behavioral patterns associated with PDA.

Collaborative Evaluation Frameworks

Collaborative evaluation frameworks involve multiple stakeholders, including individuals with PDAs, caregivers, educators, therapists, and healthcare providers. A more holistic understanding of the individual's needs and strengths can be achieved by engaging in collaborative assessments that consider diverse perspectives and expertise. This approach promotes shared decision-making and tailored interventions that address the unique challenges of PDA.

Multidisciplinary Assessment Approaches

Multidisciplinary assessment approaches involve input from professionals specializing in areas relevant to PDA, such as psychology, education, speech therapy, occupational therapy, and psychiatry. By integrating insights from multiple disciplines, a comprehensive assessment can be conducted to capture the complex nature of PDA and develop personalized support plans that address all aspects of the individual's well-being.

These tools for diagnosing and assessing PDA can empower individuals, caregivers, and professionals to make informed decisions about intervention strategies and support services. Taking a proactive approach to understanding PDA through structured assessments and collaborative evaluations makes it possible to create effective support systems tailored to the unique needs of individuals with PDA. Empowering yourself with these tools is a proactive step towards better managing the challenges associated with Pathological Demand Avoidance.

Engaging with professional organizations and communities can provide invaluable support for individuals navigating the challenges of Pathological Demand Avoidance (PDA). By connecting with these resources, readers can access specialized knowledge, guidance, and a sense of community that can significantly impact their journey towards understanding and supporting PDA. Professional organizations dedicated to neurodiversity and PDA offer a wealth of expertise and resources tailored to individuals with PDA and their families' unique needs. These organizations often host workshops, conferences, and training sessions that can enhance readers' understanding of PDAs and equip them with practical strategies for support.

Online communities centered around PDA can be a source of solace and empowerment for individuals seeking connection with others who share similar experiences. Through these virtual platforms, readers can engage in discussions, seek advice, and share their stories in a supportive environment. Joining online forums or social media groups dedicated to PDA allows readers to feel understood, validated, and less isolated in their journey.

Local support groups provide an opportunity for face-to-face interactions with individuals who have firsthand experience with PDAs. These groups often organize meetings, events, and activities that foster a sense of belonging and camaraderie among members. By participating in local support groups, readers can build meaningful relationships, exchange practical tips, and find emotional support from peers who truly understand the complexities of living with PDA.

Therapist networks specializing in PDA offer professional guidance and intervention strategies tailored to individual needs. Collaborating with therapists who are well-versed in PDA can help readers develop personalized coping mechanisms, communication strategies, and behavioral interventions that address the specific challenges associated with the condition. Therapists can also provide valuable insights into managing anxiety, sensory issues, and emotional regulation in individuals with PDA.

Parent advocacy groups are crucial in advocating for the rights and needs of individuals with PDAs within educational systems, healthcare settings, and society. By joining forces with parent advocacy groups, readers can participate in awareness campaigns, policy initiatives, and community outreach programs that aim to improve the quality of life for individuals with PDAs. These groups empower parents to advocate for their children's rights effectively and ensure their voices are heard in decision-making processes.

Research institutions conducting studies on PDA offer cutting-edge insights into the underlying mechanisms, treatment options, and best practices for supporting individuals with the condition. Keeping abreast of the latest research findings can help readers stay informed about advancements in neurodiversity and PDA management. Research institutions often publish reports, articles, and resources that provide evidence-based recommendations for professionals working with individuals diagnosed with PDA.

By engaging with professional organizations and communities dedicated to supporting individuals with PDAs, readers can access a wealth of knowledge, guidance, and emotional support essential for navigating the complexities of the condition. These resources offer a sense of belonging, empowerment, and validation that can profoundly impact readers' ability to understand and support individuals with PDAs effectively. Embracing these avenues for support enables readers to build a strong foundation of knowledge and connection that empowers them to face the challenges of PDA with resilience and compassion.

Navigating the vast landscape of resources for PDA support is not just about gathering information; it's about empowering yourself and those you care for. The tools and insights in this chapter are designed to enhance your understanding and approach to PDA, offering professional guidance and community support. By engaging with the recommended websites, online forums, and diagnostic tools, you're taking a proactive step towards more effective management and support of PDA.

Engage actively with the resources listed. Each has been carefully selected to provide comprehensive support and deeper insights into PDA. Whether you are a parent seeking guidance, an educator needing strategies, or a therapist looking to broaden your expertise, these resources are invaluable. They serve as a foundation for building knowledge and fostering connections within the PDA community.

Assessment tools are crucial for accurately identifying and understanding the nuances of PDA. Utilizing these tools can lead to better-tailored interventions that meet the unique needs of individuals. Remember, accurate diagnosis is a stepping stone towards adequate support.

Reach out to professional organizations. These bodies are not just sources of information but also hubs of advocacy and innovation in the field of PDA. Participation in these communities can provide ongoing support, up-to-date research, and networking opportunities vital for personal growth and professional development.

By taking control of your journey through these resources, you harness the power to make meaningful changes. Embrace these tools with confidence and curiosity, as they are vital to unlocking a better understanding of PDA. Remember, you are not alone in this journey; a whole community is behind each resource, ready to support and guide you.

Let this chapter serve as your springboard into a world where managing PDA becomes more accessible and less overwhelming. With each step forward, you gain more than just knowledge—you build a network of support that uplifts every member involved.

Chapter 9: Actionable Insights: Implementing Strategies Through Checklists and Templates

"Inclusion is not a matter of political correctness.

It is the key to growth."

Jesse Jackson

Transforming Insight into Action

Pathological Demand Avoidance (PDA) presents unique challenges in understanding and support, necessitating tools bridging the gap between theoretical knowledge and practical application. This chapter provides a structured approach to implementing effective strategies through checklists and templates for parents and educators dealing with PDAs. These tools are not just aids but essential components that can transform complex psychological insights into manageable, everyday actions.

Checklists and templates are vital in demystifying the steps needed to support individuals with PDAs. They offer a clear outline of actions derived from the broader principles discussed earlier in this book. These tools help caregivers and educators consistently apply the necessary interventions without feeling overwhelmed by breaking down strategies into simple, actionable tasks.

The first critical item readers will learn is how to utilize these checklists and templates effectively. Each tool provided in this chapter is crafted to guide you through specific scenarios, ensuring that no critical steps are overlooked. For instance, a morning routine checklist can help smooth out potentially stressful start-of-day transitions for someone with a PDA.

Adaptability is crucial when dealing with PDA's unpredictable nature. Therefore, the second learning outcome focuses on tailoring action plans to meet individual needs. This involves adjusting the templates provided to better suit specific situations or personal triggers that may be unique to each individual with a PDA. It's about making the tool work for you, not sticking rigidly to a preset formula.

Practical application is where theory meets reality. The third crucial element taught here is how to practice applying learned strategies in real-world settings. This isn't just about knowing what to do; it's about doing it effectively and consistently. Through examples and guided exercises, this chapter helps you translate written plans into daily routines and responses that create a supportive environment for those with PDA.

Understanding PDA requires patience and persistence, but supporting someone with this condition also demands practical wisdom—knowing what to do and when to do it. Herein lies the importance of these checklists and templates; they are more than just pieces of paper—they are stepping stones towards building competence and confidence in handling the complexities of PDA.

The design of each checklist and template included here emphasizes ease of use, encouraging users to engage actively with the material. By integrating these tools into your daily interactions, you enhance your ability to support individuals with PDAs and empower them toward greater autonomy over their challenges.

By focusing on these three key learning outcomes—utilizing tools, tailoring plans, and practicing strategies—this chapter equips readers with the knowledge. It means to make a tangible difference in the lives of those affected by Pathological Demand Avoidance. With these resources, you move beyond mere understanding towards active, effective participation in managing PDA.

Checklists and templates are invaluable tools for translating insights from the book into actionable steps that can be implemented in real-life situations. They provide a structured framework for parents and educators to follow, ensuring that strategies for supporting individuals with PDAs are effectively implemented. By utilizing these resources, individuals can turn theoretical knowledge into practical actions that directly impact the well-being of those with PDAs.

Checklists are a systematic guide, breaking down complex

strategies into manageable steps. They help organize thoughts and tasks, making tracking progress and staying focused on the end goal easier. With checklists, individuals can ensure that no crucial step is missed, leading to a more comprehensive implementation of supportive strategies. These tools act as a roadmap, guiding users through each action plan stage promoting consistency and thoroughness in their approach.

Templates provide a standardized format for structuring action plans tailored to specific needs. They offer a starting point for customization, allowing individuals to adapt strategies based on unique circumstances. Templates streamline the development of action plans by outlining key components such as goals, timelines, and resources needed. Using templates, parents and educators can save time and effort in creating detailed plans that address the diverse challenges associated with PDAs.

Combining checklists and templates creates a dynamic approach to implementing strategies for individuals with PDAs. Checklists ensure that all necessary tasks are completed, while templates offer a blueprint for designing personalized action plans. This synergy enhances the efficiency and effectiveness of support strategies, enabling smoother execution and better outcomes for individuals with PDAs.

Crafting Personalized Action Plans for Supporting Individuals with Pathological Demand Avoidance (PDA)

Implementing supportive strategies for individuals with Pathological Demand Avoidance (PDA) requires tailored action plans that cater to the unique needs and challenges of each individual. Personalization is critical when creating these plans, as what works for one person with a PDA may not be effective for another. By customizing strategies to fit the specific characteristics and triggers of the individual with a PDA, parents, and educators can increase the likelihood of success in managing behaviors and fostering positive outcomes.

When tailoring action plans, observing and understanding the individual's responses to different situations is essential. By keeping track of what triggers anxiety or meltdowns and noting successful interventions, caregivers can develop a comprehensive plan that addresses the individual's specific needs. Flexibility is crucial in adapting these action plans as behaviors evolve or new challenges arise, ensuring that support remains effective over time.

In creating tailored action plans, involving the individual with PDA is essential whenever possible. By collaborating with them and considering their preferences and perspectives, caregivers can create a plan more likely to be embraced and followed by the individual. Empowering them to participate in decision-making about their support strategies can also foster a sense of autonomy and self-efficacy.

Another critical aspect of tailoring action plans for individuals with PDA is consistency. By establishing clear routines and expectations, caregivers can provide a structured environment that reduces anxiety and uncertainty for the individual. Consistent implementation of support strategies across different settings can also reinforce positive behaviors and facilitate the generalization of skills.

Incorporating positive reinforcement into action plans is essential for individuals with PDA. By rewarding desired behaviors and efforts, caregivers can motivate the individual to continue engaging in adaptive behaviors and following the established support strategies. Acknowledging progress, no matter how small, can boost self-esteem and encourage continued growth.

When tailoring action plans for individuals with PDA, it is important to prioritize self-care for caregivers. Supporting individuals with PDA can be demanding, both emotionally and physically. Caregivers must ensure they take breaks, seek support from others, and practice self-compassion to maintain their well-being while implementing these strategies effectively.

Action Implementation Framework: Navigating Support Strategies for Individuals with PDA

The Action Implementation Framework outlined in this section serves as a structured guide for readers to effectively translate the insights and strategies discussed in the book into practical actions within their daily environments. This framework aims to facilitate the application of supportive strategies for individuals with Pathological Demand Avoidance (PDA) by providing a step-by-step approach that emphasizes actionable steps and continuous reflection on progress.

Current Situation Evaluation

The framework's first step involves evaluating the individual's current situation with a PDA. This evaluation helps identify specific challenges and areas of improvement, laying the foundation for tailored support strategies. By understanding the unique needs and capabilities of the individual, parents, and educators can develop targeted interventions that address their concerns effectively.

SMART Goal Setting

Following the evaluation phase, readers are encouraged to set

SMART goals: Specific, Measurable, Achievable, Relevant, and Time-bound objectives that align with the identified challenges. SMART goals provide a clear roadmap for progress and ensure that interventions are purposeful and attainable within a specified timeframe. By setting precise objectives, individuals can track their achievements and stay motivated throughout the implementation process.

Action Plan Development

Once SMART goals are established, readers can develop action plans incorporating recommended interventions from previous chapters. These action plans should be gradual and tailored to the individual's needs, focusing on implementing supportive strategies in a structured manner to avoid overwhelming them. By breaking down complex tasks into manageable steps, parents and educators can facilitate smoother transitions and foster positive outcomes for individuals with PDA.

Monitoring Progress

The monitoring phase is an integral part of the framework, where progress is tracked, and action plans are adjusted as necessary. Regular monitoring allows course corrections and ensures that interventions address the individual's evolving needs effectively. Parents and educators can fine-tune their support strategies for optimal results by staying vigilant and responsive to changes.

Reflection and Iteration

The framework emphasizes a cycle of reflection and iteration, encouraging readers to continually learn from their experiences and refine their approaches. By reflecting on successes and challenges, individuals can gain valuable insights into what works best for them or their child with PDA. This iterative process promotes growth and adaptation, leading to more effective support structures.

Application Scenarios

To enhance practical understanding, hypothetical scenarios or case studies are included to demonstrate how the framework can be applied in real-life situations. These examples offer concrete illustrations of adaptable support strategies in action, showcasing the flexibility and efficacy of the framework in diverse contexts. By engaging with these scenarios, readers can better visualize how to implement strategies tailored to their unique circumstances.

The Action Implementation Framework provides a systematic approach to implementing supportive strategies for individuals with PDAs. By guiding readers through evaluation, goal setting, action planning, monitoring progress, reflection, iteration, and practical application scenarios, this framework equips parents and educators with a comprehensive toolkit for navigating the challenges associated with PDA effectively.

In this chapter, we have explored the power of checklists and templates to transform theoretical insights into practical, actionable steps. These tools are not merely organizational aids but instrumental in fostering an environment where individuals with PDAs can thrive. By tailoring action plans to meet unique needs, you empower yourself and the individuals you support, ensuring that interventions are meaningful and effective.

The importance of practicing these strategies in everyday situations cannot be overstated. It is through consistent application that theoretical knowledge is converted into real-world skills, enhancing your ability to provide empathetic and practical support. Remember, each small step using these strategies builds towards greater understanding and more effective support.

Take control of your situation. You have the tools to make significant changes in how you support individuals with PDAs. Each checklist and template is designed to be easy to implement, reducing overwhelming feelings and increasing your confidence in handling challenging scenarios.

Let these tools guide you as you navigate the complexities of supporting unique minds. With each action you take, you are applying what you've learned and setting a foundation for continuous improvement and deeper connection.

Remember, your journey with PDA is not just about managing challenges but also about celebrating every victory, no matter how small. Your efforts make a profound difference in the lives of those you support, allowing them to express their true selves in a supportive environment.

By actively engaging with the strategies outlined here, you enhance your understanding while providing invaluable support that respects each person's individuality with PDA. Let's move forward together, equipped with knowledge and tools to meet challenges head-on while fostering an atmosphere of acceptance and growth.

Chapter 10: Clarifying Questions: Expert Answers to Common PDA Queries

"The real voyage of discovery consists not in seeking new landscapes, but in having new eyes."

Marcel Proust

Are You Navigating the Complexities of PDA? Get Expert Answers Now

Pathological Demand Avoidance (PDA) is a complex and often misunderstood aspect of the autism spectrum that challenges conventional understanding and management strategies. This chapter aims to bridge the gap between confusion and clarity by addressing the most common questions surrounding PDAs with expertise and compassion. Here, we delve into expert responses that shed light on PDA, aiming to dispel prevalent myths and clarify this condition.

Many families, educators, and health professionals grapple with misconceptions about PDAs. These include doubts about its validity as a diagnosis, misunderstandings about its symptoms, and confusion over effective management strategies. By bringing together insights from leading experts in the field, this chapter provides authoritative answers that clarify these issues and offer practical advice for those dealing with PDAs in their lives or work.

The necessity for accurate information cannot be overstated. Misinformation leads to approaches that can exacerbate the challenges faced by individuals with PDA. Therefore, it is crucial to approach PDA with strategies tailored to its unique demands. This includes understanding why conventional discipline methods often fail and recognizing the importance of negotiation and interaction flexibility.

A significant portion of this chapter is dedicated to explaining why individuals with PDA exhibit strong resistance to everyday demands and how this is not a choice but rather a part of their neurology. Experts clarify that this isn't about being difficult but about an anxiety-driven need to control their environment to feel secure. Recognizing this can transform how parents, teachers, and peers respond to someone with PDA.

Furthermore, practical strategies are discussed extensively here. From creating environments that reduce demand triggers to communication techniques that foster cooperation rather than conflict, readers will find actionable advice grounded in real-world applications. These strategies emphasize respect for the individual's needs and capabilities, encouraging a supportive rather than confrontational approach.

Empowerment through knowledge is a recurring theme throughout our discussion. Understanding PDA deeply empowers parents, educators, and healthcare professionals to make informed decisions that enhance their ability to support individuals effectively. It also empowers those with PDAs, offering them insights into their behavior patterns, which can be crucial for self-management and advocacy.

Lastly, by demystifying PDA through expert dialogue, we aim to foster a community that is better informed and more empathetic towards variability in human behavior. This not only aids in creating supportive environments but also promotes acceptance and inclusion for individuals with PDA.

This chapter serves as an essential conduit for accurate information, robust support strategies, and compassionate understanding—all vital tools for anyone looking to successfully navigate the complexities of Pathological Demand Avoidance.

Addressing common questions and misconceptions about Pathological Demand Avoidance (PDA) is essential to provide clarity and understanding for individuals navigating this complex condition. Experts in the field offer valuable insights to illuminate common queries and dispel myths surrounding PDAs. One common misconception is that individuals with PDA are simply being oppositional or defiant. However, it's crucial to recognize that PDA is a neurodevelopmental condition that requires a nuanced approach for adequate support.

Experts emphasize the importance of understanding PDA as a profile within the autism spectrum, characterized by an extreme anxiety-driven need to be in control. This need for control can manifest as avoidance of demands, leading to challenging behaviors. By acknowledging the underlying anxiety and need for control, caregivers and educators can tailor their approaches to better support individuals with PDAs. Empathy and flexibility are critical components in building positive relationships with individuals with PDA, fostering trust and cooperation.

Another common question revolves around the difference between PDA and other forms of autism. Experts clarify that while there are overlapping traits between PDA and other autism spectrum disorders, such as social communication difficulties, the central feature of PDA is the avoidance of everyday demands perceived as threatening. Understanding this core aspect of PDA can guide interventions that focus on reducing demands and providing predictability and choice to alleviate anxiety.

Practical strategies experts recommend include using visual supports to enhance communication, offering structured routines to provide predictability, and implementing positive reinforcement techniques to encourage desired behaviors. Creating an environment that minimizes demands while promoting autonomy can help individuals with PDA feel more secure and in control, reducing anxiety levels and challenging behaviors.

Caregivers, educators, and professionals must educate themselves about PDAs to offer appropriate support and understanding. By dispelling myths and addressing common questions with expert insights, individuals can develop a deeper appreciation for the unique challenges faced by those with PDAs. Through empathy, flexibility, and tailored strategies, it is possible to create supportive environments where individuals with PDA can thrive.

Dispelling Myths and Understanding Realities of Pathological Demand Avoidance (PDA)

PDA, or Pathological Demand Avoidance, can be a complex concept for both individuals experiencing it and those trying to understand and support them. Misconceptions often cloud the understanding of PDA, leading to confusion and frustration. One common myth surrounding PDA is that individuals who exhibit this behavior are simply being oppositional or defiant. In reality, PDA stems from an anxiety-driven need to avoid demands that can overwhelm the individual rather than a deliberate act of defiance.

To clarify, it's essential to recognize that individuals with PDA may struggle with traditional strategies used for other forms of autism spectrum disorders. The nature of PDA requires a more nuanced approach that acknowledges the underlying anxieties and difficulties in coping with everyday demands. By reframing the perspective on challenging behaviors associated with PDA as coping mechanisms rather than intentional defiance, it becomes easier to provide the appropriate support and understanding needed.

Another misconception is that individuals with PDAs can "snap out of it" or conform to expectations if pushed hard enough. The truth is trying too hard can exacerbate anxiety levels and lead to more challenging behaviors. Understanding the triggers and adapting communication and support strategies are critical components in effectively managing PDA. By acknowledging the unique needs of individuals with PDAs and providing a supportive environment that minimizes overwhelming demands, progress can be made toward positive outcomes.

It's crucial to dispel the myth that individuals with PDA are intentionally manipulative or controlling. These behaviors often stem from a deep-seated fear of failure or inability to meet expectations rather than a desire for control over others. By fostering a compassionate and understanding approach, building trust and rapport with individuals with PDA is possible, creating a foundation for effective communication and support.

Understanding the complexities of PDA requires a shift in perspective from viewing behaviors as intentional defiance to recognizing them as manifestations of underlying anxiety and difficulties in managing demands. By adopting strategies tailored to address these specific needs, individuals with PDAs can receive the support they require to navigate daily challenges more effectively. Dispelling myths surrounding PDA is essential in promoting accurate understanding and fostering environments conducive to growth and development for individuals facing this condition.

In supporting individuals with PDAs, practical guidance is crucial in navigating the challenges that may arise. Understanding the unique needs of individuals with PDAs is foundational to providing practical support. One key aspect is establishing clear communication strategies catering to their preferences and sensitivities. Active listening and empathetic responses can foster trust and understanding, creating a conducive environment for effective communication.

Tailoring environments to accommodate sensory sensitivities is another vital aspect of supporting individuals with PDA. Creating spaces that minimize sensory overload can significantly reduce stress and anxiety levels. Dimming lights, providing noise-canceling headphones, or offering fidget tools are simple yet impactful ways to create sensory-friendly environments.

Establishing routines and clear expectations can provide a sense of predictability and structure for individuals with PDAs. Consistent schedules and visual supports, such as calendars or checklists, can help individuals navigate daily tasks more effectively. Flexibility within routines is also essential to accommodate each individual's unique needs and preferences.

Building a support network that includes professionals, family members, educators, and peers is crucial in providing comprehensive support for individuals with PDAs. Collaborating with experts in the field can offer valuable insights and strategies tailored to the individual's specific needs. Seeking guidance from occupational therapists, behavior analysts, or special education teachers can enhance the quality of support provided.

Positive reinforcement strategies can effectively promote desired behaviors and reduce challenging ones. Acknowledging small successes and celebrating achievements can motivate individuals with PDA to continue working towards their goals. Reward systems, such as token economies or praise charts, can effectively reinforce positive behaviors.

Encouraging self-regulation techniques empowers individuals with PDA to manage their emotions and behaviors effectively. Teaching relaxation strategies, such as deep breathing exercises or mindfulness techniques, can help individuals cope with stress and anxiety in various situations. Modeling self-regulation by practicing these techniques can also be a powerful example for individuals with PDAs.

Lastly, fostering a strengths-based approach emphasizes individuals' unique abilities and talents with PDA rather than focusing solely on challenges. Recognizing and nurturing their strengths, whether in creative pursuits, problem-solving skills, or special interests, can boost their confidence and self-esteem. Embracing a holistic view that appreciates the individual can create a supportive environment where they can thrive.

By implementing these practical strategies and approaches, caregivers, educators, and support providers can create an inclusive and empowering environment for individuals with PDAs to flourish. Each step towards understanding their unique needs and providing tailored support contributes to building a more supportive community for individuals with PDAs.

Through the focused dialogue in this chapter, we have endeavored to address common questions and misconceptions about PDAs with precision and care. Expert insights have been crucial in offering answers and dispelling prevalent myths that often obscure understanding of PDA. This approach ensures that you, as a reader, are equipped with the most accurate and actionable information available.

Understanding PDA is fundamental, and through these discussions, we aim to provide a solid foundation upon which individuals can build effective support mechanisms. By clarifying these complex issues with straightforward explanations, we empower you to take informed actions to improve daily interactions and long-term outcomes significantly.

For those directly or indirectly affected by PDA, this chapter serves as a reassuring reminder that you are not alone in your journey. There are practical strategies and real-world advice that can be implemented immediately, fostering an environment of support and understanding.

We encourage you to engage with the strategies discussed here actively. The path to mastery over PDA's challenges is not merely theoretical but involves the hands-on application of shared knowledge. Embrace these tools confidently, knowing they are rooted in expert research and tailored to provide relief and direction in navigating PDA.

As we progress in this book, remember that each step taken to understand PDA is a stride toward empowerment. Your engagement with this material is not just for knowledge but for actionable change that can transform lives. Let's continue this path together, armed with insights and ready to make a positive impact.

Chapter 11: A Compassionate Approach: Strategies for Siblings and Peers

"The only way to make sense out of change

is to plunge into it, move with it,

and join the dance."

Alan Watts

Empathy in Action: Supporting Siblings and Peers

Understanding and supporting a family member or friend with Pathological Demand Avoidance (PDA) requires more than good intentions; it demands a compassionate, informed approach. The challenges faced by individuals with PDA are unique and often misunderstood, leading to complex dynamics within family and peer groups. This chapter aims to equip siblings and peers with the necessary tools to foster inclusive, supportive relationships that acknowledge these challenges and actively work to alleviate them.

The first step in this journey is education. Peers and siblings must understand the fundamental aspects of PDA, such as its manifestation in behaviors that may initially appear as stubbornness or manipulation. These behaviors, however, are rooted in intense anxiety and a need to avoid everyday demands due to an overwhelming sense of losing control. By grasping this concept, siblings and peers can shift their perspectives from frustration to empathy.

Building on this foundation of understanding, the next focus is on developing effective communication strategies. Siblings and peers need to learn how to approach their loved ones with PDA in a way that minimizes perceived demands. Simple adjustments in language and approach can make a significant difference. For instance, offering choices instead of direct commands can help individuals with PDA feel more in control, thus reducing their anxiety and oppositional responses.

In addition to modifying communication tactics, creating a supportive environment is crucial. This involves being mindful of the need for flexibility and adaptability in plans and expectations. Siblings and peers play a pivotal role here; they can advocate for environments where the individual with PDA feels safe and understood, whether at home, school, or social gatherings.

Furthermore, fostering inclusive relationships extends beyond the immediate family or friendship circle. It involves educating others about PDA to promote understanding and acceptance in wider social networks. Siblings and peers can be powerful advocates in schools and communities by sharing their insights and experiences.

To navigate these social dynamics effectively, it's essential for siblings and peers also to take care of their emotional well-being. Supporting someone with PDA can be challenging, and acknowledging this isn't an admission of failure but a step towards building resilience. Seeking support from parents, professionals, or support groups can provide additional coping strategies and emotional relief.

Lastly, mutual respect is the cornerstone of any relationship. For siblings and peers of individuals with PDA, practicing patience and showing consistent support can strengthen bonds significantly. It's about celebrating successes, no matter how small, and recognizing the effort it takes for someone with PDA to manage their day-to-day life.

Through these strategies—education, effective communication, creating supportive environments, advocacy for inclusion, self-care for supporters, and mutual respect—siblings and peers can significantly impact the lives of individuals with PDA. By adopting these approaches, they not only improve the quality of life for their loved ones but also enrich their own experiences through deeper connections and understanding.

Navigating the complexities of supporting a family member or friend with Pathological Demand Avoidance (PDA) can be challenging, especially for siblings and peers who may not fully understand the condition. It's crucial to approach this situation with empathy and an open mind to provide support. Here are some practical tips and advice for siblings and peers on understanding and assisting individuals with PDAs:

1. Educate Yourself: Understanding is the first step towards adequate support. Take the time to educate yourself about PDA, its characteristics, and how it manifests in daily life. Knowledge is critical to fostering empathy and creating a supportive environment.

2. Communicate Openly: Communication is essential in any relationship. Encourage open dialogue with your sibling or friend with a PDA. Listen attentively, ask questions, and express your willingness to understand their perspective. Clear communication can help build trust and strengthen your bond.

3. Be Patient: Patience is a virtue when supporting someone with a PDA. Individuals with PDA may struggle with flexibility and transitions, leading to challenging behaviors. Stay calm, be patient, and offer reassurance during challenging moments.

4. Offer Predictability: Consistency can provide a sense of security. Establishing routines and providing predictability can help reduce anxiety for individuals with PDA. Offer clear expectations and communicate any changes in advance to minimize stress.

5. Respect Boundaries: Respecting personal boundaries is crucial.

Individuals with PDA may have specific triggers or sensitivities. Be mindful of their boundaries, respect their need for space when required, and avoid overwhelming them with demands.

6. Celebrate Achievements: Acknowledge and celebrate small victories. Encouragement and positive reinforcement can motivate individuals with PDA. Recognize their efforts, no matter how small, to boost their self-esteem and confidence.

7. Seek Support Together: You mustn't navigate this journey alone. Encourage your sibling or friend with a PDA to seek professional support if needed. Therapy sessions or support groups can enhance understanding and strengthen your relationship.

Fostering Inclusive Relationships and Compassion in Family and Peer Circles

In fostering inclusive relationships and compassion among family and friends, it is essential to approach the situation with understanding and empathy. Acknowledge that each individual's experience is unique, and it's crucial to create a supportive environment where everyone feels heard and valued. Encouraging open communication can help bridge gaps in understanding and strengthen bonds between siblings and peers.

Empathy is critical in nurturing relationships. One can better comprehend their perspective and challenges by putting oneself in the shoes of a sibling or friend with a PDA. Listening actively without judgment can foster trust and create a safe space for sharing thoughts and emotions. Validating their feelings and experiences can go a long way in building a supportive network.

Practicing patience is fundamental when supporting a family member or friend with a PDA. Understand that progress may be gradual, and setbacks are natural. Consistent support and encouragement can empower individuals with PDAs to navigate social interactions more confidently. Celebrate small victories together, reinforcing positive behaviors and accomplishments.

To cultivate compassion among siblings and peers, educate them about PDA. Providing information about the condition can dispel misconceptions and promote acceptance. Encourage open dialogue where questions can be asked without hesitation, fostering an environment of learning and understanding.

Promote inclusivity within social circles by organizing activities that cater to everyone's needs and preferences. Consider individual sensitivities and interests when planning gatherings or outings. Encourage cooperation and teamwork, emphasizing the value of collaboration in building solid relationships.

Supporting a family member or friend with a PDA requires flexibility and adaptability. Be prepared to adjust plans or routines to accommodate their needs comfortably. Please respect their boundaries, allowing them space when necessary while being available for support when required.

In nurturing compassionate relationships, emphasize the importance of kindness. Small acts of kindness can make a significant impact on someone's day, fostering positivity within relationships. Encourage siblings and peers to express gratitude and appreciation for each other regularly.

By fostering inclusive relationships built on compassion, understanding, and support, siblings and peers can create a nurturing environment where individuals with PDA feel accepted, valued, and empowered. Together, they can navigate challenges, celebrate successes, and cultivate strong bonds that withstand the test of time.

Navigating social dynamics and enhancing mutual respect and understanding within peer groups is essential when supporting individuals with Pathological Demand Avoidance (PDA). Encouraging open communication among peers and siblings can lead to a more inclusive and compassionate environment. Promoting empathy and understanding individuals' unique challenges with PDA can foster stronger relationships within peer groups.

Creating awareness about PDA among peers is crucial in promoting acceptance and support. Educating friends and classmates about the characteristics of PDA can reduce misunderstandings and encourage empathy. Encouraging open discussions about how best to support a friend or family member with a PDA can lead to more effective strategies for inclusion.

Setting boundaries within peer groups is essential to ensure that individuals with PDAs feel respected and understood. Establishing clear guidelines on how to communicate and interact with someone with PDA can prevent conflicts and foster a supportive environment. Encouraging patience and flexibility when engaging with individuals with PDA can lead to more positive interactions and stronger relationships.

Promoting collaboration within peer groups can enhance mutual respect and understanding. Encouraging peers to work together to support their friend or family member with PDA can create a sense of unity and shared responsibility. Fostering a community where everyone feels valued and included can lead to more positive social interactions for individuals with PDAs.

Emphasizing the importance of listening and validating the feelings of individuals with PDA can strengthen relationships within peer groups. Showing empathy and offering support without judgment can create a safe space for individuals with PDAs to express themselves openly. Encouraging peers to practice active listening and respond with compassion can deepen connections and build trust.

Modeling inclusive behavior within peer groups is critical to promoting understanding and respect for individuals with PDA. Demonstrating acceptance, empathy, and kindness towards others sets a positive example for interacting with someone with unique needs. Encouraging peers to be supportive allies can create a more welcoming environment for everyone.

In summary, navigating social dynamics and enhancing mutual respect within peer groups involves creating awareness, setting boundaries, promoting collaboration, emphasizing listening, and modeling inclusive behavior. By fostering an environment of understanding, empathy, and support, peers can play a vital role in creating a positive experience for individuals with PDA in social settings.

Understanding and supporting a family member or friend with PDA requires patience, knowledge, and a great deal of compassion. By sharing practical advice on fostering inclusive relationships, this chapter aims to equip siblings and peers with the tools they need to enhance their interactions and deepen their understanding of those affected by PDA.

Navigating the social dynamics within families and peer groups can often seem challenging, but with the right strategies, it becomes manageable. Encouraging open communication and educating oneself about PDA are crucial steps in creating an environment where every individual feels respected and valued. Remember, practical support stems from a genuine attempt to understand the unique challenges faced by individuals with PDAs.

The ability to foster inclusive relationships benefits the individual with PDA and enriches the lives of all involved. By embracing differences and practicing empathy, siblings, and peers can cultivate a supportive network that stands firm in facing challenges. This not only aids in reducing misunderstandings but also promotes a sense of belonging and acceptance.

Taking actionable steps toward understanding and support does not require grand gestures; small acts of kindness and acceptance often make the most significant impact. Therefore, engage actively with the strategies discussed, applying them consistently in daily interactions.

By implementing these compassionate approaches, you empower yourself and others to build more robust, understanding relationships that uphold dignity and respect for everyone. This proactive involvement is vital to overcoming obstacles and fostering an environment where unique minds thrive. So, take control of your role as a sibling or peer—your actions can lead to meaningful change in managing social dynamics around PDA.

Chapter 12: The Caregiver's Journey: Self-Care and Emotional Support

"To understand and be understood, those are among

life's greatest gifts, and every interaction is an

opportunity to exchange them."

Maria Popova

When the Caregiver Needs Care

Supporting a child or family member with Pathological Demand Avoidance (PDA) is profoundly rewarding yet uniquely challenging. Often, caregivers pour their energy into meeting the complex needs of their loved ones, inadvertently sidelining their well-being. This oversight can lead to burnout and emotional, physical, and mental exhaustion caused by prolonged stress. Recognizing the signs of caregiver fatigue is crucial; it's beneficial and essential for sustainable caregiving.

The primary step in preventing burnout is acknowledging that caregiver health directly influences their ability to provide care. Stress and exhaustion can cloud judgment, reduce empathy, and ultimately impair the caregiver's effectiveness. Therefore, prioritizing self-care isn't an act of selfishness but a strategic component of effective caregiving. Integrating regular periods of rest and recovery into one's routine is vital.

Strategies for maintaining emotional health are diverse and can be tailored to fit individual lifestyles and preferences. Simple practices such as mindfulness meditation, regular physical activity, and engaging in hobbies can significantly alleviate stress. Additionally, setting boundaries is crucial; it's okay to say no or to delegate tasks when possible. These strategies help maintain the caregiver's health and model healthy coping mechanisms for those they care for.

Support systems play a pivotal role in a caregiver's life. Connecting with other caregivers who understand the unique challenges of living with someone with PDA can provide emotional solace and practical advice. Various online communities and local support groups offer spaces where experiences and resources are shared freely, fostering a sense of community and mutual support.

Creating a culture of self-awareness among caregivers involves recognizing personal limits and understanding when to seek help. Caregivers need to monitor their emotional states and acknowledge feelings of sadness, frustration, or anger without guilt. Accepting these emotions as valid responses to stressful situations rather than signs of weakness enables caregivers to address them constructively.

Mindfulness enhances this self-awareness, allowing caregivers to remain present and engaged with their loved ones without becoming overwhelmed by future worries or past regrets. Mindfulness techniques can seamlessly integrate into daily routines, offering a practical method for managing stress in real time.

Lastly, caregivers must maintain perspective regarding their journey. The role they play is indispensable—not only in the mechanics of daily care but in shaping the psychological and emotional environment around their loved one with PDA. By taking care of themselves, caregivers are better equipped to foster a nurturing, supportive space that promotes growth and development for themselves and their loved ones.

Through these approaches—prioritizing self-care, leveraging support systems, and fostering self-awareness through mindfulness—caregivers can find resilience amidst challenges. Engaging actively with these strategies ensures they are prepared for the long-term caregiving journey while safeguarding their emotional well-being.

As parents and caregivers navigate the intricate landscape of PDA, it is crucial to recognize the significance of self-care and emotional well-being. The journey of supporting individuals with PDA can be demanding, both physically and emotionally. Taking care of oneself is not a luxury but a necessity, as it equips caregivers with the resilience needed to provide practical support in the long run. Neglecting self-care can lead to burnout, impacting the caregiver's well-being and the quality of care provided to their loved ones.

Self-care is not selfish; it is a vital component of sustainable caregiving. It involves setting boundaries, prioritizing personal needs, and seeking necessary support. By nurturing their well-being, caregivers can better attend to the needs of individuals with PDAs. Engaging in activities that bring joy, practicing mindfulness, and seeking respite are all essential aspects of self-care that can prevent exhaustion and maintain emotional balance.

Emotional well-being is at the core of effective caregiving. It is usual for caregivers to experience a range of emotions, from joy and fulfillment to frustration and overwhelm. Acknowledging these emotions without judgment is critical to maintaining emotional health. Seeking outlets for expression, such as talking to a trusted friend or therapist, can help process complex feelings and prevent them from festering.

Remember that you are not alone in this journey. Reach out to support groups, online forums, or local organizations that cater to caregivers of individuals with PDAs. Connecting with others who understand your challenges can provide a sense of belonging and validation. Sharing experiences and strategies with fellow caregivers can offer valuable insights and emotional support.

Cultivating Resilience and Finding Support in Caregiving

Caregiving can be emotionally taxing, requiring resilience and support to navigate its challenges effectively. As caregivers, it is crucial to prioritize your well-being to ensure you can provide the best care for your loved ones. Here are some practical strategies and resources to help you build resilience and find the support you need.

1. Seek Support Networks: Connecting with other caregivers who understand your experiences can provide a sense of belonging and validation. Joining support groups in person or online can offer a safe space to share your feelings and gain insights from others facing similar situations.

2. Practice Self-Care: Taking care of yourself is not selfish; it is essential for maintaining mental and emotional health. Make time for activities that bring you joy and relaxation, whether reading a book, going for a walk, or indulging in a hobby. Prioritize self-care routines to recharge your energy levels and reduce stress.

3. Set Boundaries: Establishing boundaries is crucial in maintaining a healthy balance between caregiving responsibilities and personal needs. Learn to say no when necessary, delegate tasks when possible, and communicate your limits to others involved in caregiving.

4. Educate Yourself: Knowledge is empowering, especially when

understanding the condition or challenges your loved one is facing. Stay informed about relevant topics through reputable sources, attend workshops or seminars, and consult with professionals to enhance your caregiving skills.

5. Utilize Respite Care: Don't hesitate to ask for help. Respite care services can provide temporary relief by offering professional assistance in caring for your loved one. Taking breaks is essential for recharging your energy and preventing burnout.

6. Practice Mindfulness: Mindfulness techniques can help you stay present in the moment and manage stress effectively. Engage in activities such as meditation, deep breathing exercises, or yoga to promote relaxation and mental clarity amidst the challenges of caregiving.

7. Maintain Healthy Relationships: Nurturing positive relationships with friends and family members can provide emotional support during difficult times. Don't hesitate to seek help or spend quality time with loved ones who uplift and encourage you.

Implementing these strategies into your caregiving routine can enhance your resilience, prioritize your well-being, and navigate the caregiving journey with greater strength and emotional balance. Remember that caring for yourself is not a luxury but a necessity in providing sustainable care for those you love.

Creating a culture of self-awareness and mindfulness is essential for sustaining long-term engagement in caring roles. Self-awareness involves recognizing one's own emotions, thoughts, and values, while mindfulness focuses on being present in the moment without judgment. By cultivating these practices, caregivers can better navigate their challenges and support their loved ones more effectively with PDAs.

Practicing self-awareness allows caregivers to acknowledge their own needs and limitations. It is crucial to prioritize self-care and recognize when to step back and recharge. This might involve setting boundaries, seeking support from others, or engaging in activities that bring joy and relaxation. Understanding one's emotional state enables caregivers to respond more thoughtfully to tricky situations and prevent burnout.

Mindfulness plays a vital role in maintaining emotional balance amidst the demands of caregiving. Caregivers can reduce stress and anxiety by staying present and focused on the task. Mindfulness techniques such as deep breathing, meditation, or grounding exercises can help caregivers center themselves during challenging moments. This practice enhances resilience and promotes a sense of calm in the face of adversity.

Incorporating self-care routines into daily life is essential for caregivers to sustain their well-being over time. Simple acts of self-compassion, such as taking short breaks, engaging in physical activity, or connecting with supportive individuals, can make a significant difference in how caregivers feel and function. It is not selfish to prioritize self-care; it is an investment in one's ability to provide adequate care in the long run.

Building a support network is another crucial aspect of creating a culture of self-awareness and mindfulness. Connecting with other caregivers who understand the challenges firsthand can provide validation, encouragement, and practical tips for coping with stress. Online forums, support groups, or therapy sessions can offer valuable resources for caregivers seeking emotional support and camaraderie.

By fostering a growth mindset and continuous learning, caregivers can adapt to new challenges and cultivate resilience. Embracing change as an opportunity for personal development allows caregivers to approach difficulties with a sense of curiosity rather than fear. Each obstacle becomes a chance to learn more about oneself and develop new coping strategies for future obstacles.

Practicing gratitude is a powerful way to cultivate mindfulness and appreciation for the positives in life. By focusing on what brings joy, fulfillment, and meaning, caregivers can shift their perspective from scarcity to abundance. Expressing gratitude for small moments of connection or progress can boost emotional well-being and foster a sense of hope during challenging times.

In summary, creating a culture of self-awareness and mindfulness involves prioritizing self-care, building a support network, embracing a growth mindset, practicing gratitude, and staying present. By incorporating these practices into daily life, caregivers can sustain their emotional well-being while providing compassionate care to individuals with PDAs.

The caregiving journey is challenging and rewarding, particularly for those supporting individuals with unique minds. It necessitates a deep commitment to self-care and emotional well-being. Self-care is not just a luxury but a crucial aspect of maintaining your ability to provide adequate support over the long term. Remember, prioritizing your health and emotional needs directly impacts your ability to care for others.

Strategies such as setting clear boundaries, seeking supportive communities, and engaging in regular mindfulness practices are not merely suggestions; they are essential tools that foster resilience. These strategies empower you to handle the stresses of caregiving roles more effectively. Adopting these practices creates a sustainable path that benefits you and those you care for.

Creating a culture of self-awareness and mindfulness within your caregiving environment helps cultivate patience and empathy, which are vital in managing day-to-day challenges. Regular reflection on personal experiences and feelings can significantly enhance your understanding and responsiveness to the needs of those you support.

Take control of your caregiving journey by actively engaging with these resources and strategies. Your role is indispensable, and your well-being is fundamental to your effectiveness. Embrace these tools with confidence, knowing that each step you take in fostering your resilience strengthens your capacity to be an extraordinary caregiver.

Let this chapter remind you that you are not alone in this journey. There is strength in seeking help and learning from others who share similar experiences. Together, through understanding and support, overcoming the challenges of caregiving becomes a possibility and a reality.

Chapter 13: Advocacy and Awareness: Navigating Social and Legal Landscapes

"When you judge someone based on a diagnosis, you miss out

on their abilities, beauty, and uniqueness."

Unknown

Shaping the Future Through Understanding and Action

Pathological Demand Avoidance (PDA) is a complex profile that calls for a nuanced approach, especially regarding advocacy and navigating legal and social landscapes. This chapter delves into the essential strategies and considerations that can empower families, educators, and individuals to support those with PDAs effectively.

Advocacy is not just about speaking up; it's about speaking right. For individuals with PDA, whose needs are often misunderstood or overlooked, effective advocacy involves a deep understanding of the condition combined with strategic communication. Readers will learn how to craft messages that resonate with policymakers, educators, and the community, ensuring that these messages lead to meaningful change.

The legal landscape surrounding disabilities can be daunting. However, knowing one's rights is crucial for securing accommodations and support. This section of the chapter breaks down the relevant laws and regulations in a way that is easy to understand. It provides actionable advice on navigating these systems to advocate for appropriate educational settings and other accommodations that respect the unique needs of those with PDAs.

Moreover, social understanding plays a pivotal role in shaping the experiences of individuals with PDAs. Misconceptions and stigma can isolate these individuals and limit their opportunities. This chapter offers practical tips on educating others, managing public perceptions, and fostering inclusive environments in educational settings and within broader communities.

Empowerment through knowledge is a recurring theme here. Equipping readers with the right tools and understanding can make them confident advocates who initiate real-world changes. Whether it's through setting up awareness campaigns, participating in school meetings, or simply sharing experiences with others, every action counts.

Navigating social situations requires tact and sensitivity. For people with PDA, unexpected demands can trigger extreme anxiety or meltdowns. Readers will gain insights into how to prepare for various social interactions, advocate for accommodations in public spaces, and educate those around them about PDAs in a way that promotes empathy and support.

Finally, empowerment is about turning challenges into opportunities for growth. This chapter educates and inspires readers to embrace their role as advocates—with the power to influence both small-scale interactions and broader societal views on PDAs.

Through straightforward language, this chapter arms readers with knowledge while encouraging them to take active steps toward creating a more understanding and accommodating world for those with Pathological Demand Avoidance.

Navigating the social and legal landscapes surrounding Pathological Demand Avoidance (PDA) can be a challenging task, requiring a combination of advocacy and awareness. As individuals with PDA often face misconceptions and lack of understanding in various settings, it becomes crucial to equip oneself with strategies to advocate effectively and raise awareness about this unique profile.

Advocacy Strategies: One key aspect of navigating the social and legal landscapes for individuals with PDA involves developing effective advocacy strategies. Empowering oneself with knowledge about PDA, its characteristics, and how it differs from other conditions on the autism spectrum can be a foundational step. Seeking support from professionals who are familiar with PDAs and can provide guidance on advocating for appropriate accommodations in various environments is essential. Building a solid support network comprising family, friends, educators, and therapists who understand PDA can bolster advocacy efforts.

Raising Awareness: In addition to advocating for individual needs, raising awareness about PDA in broader social circles is crucial. Educating others about the specific challenges individuals face with PDA can help dispel misconceptions and foster understanding. Organizing community events or workshops to spread awareness about PDA, its symptoms, and practical support strategies can contribute to creating more inclusive environments. Utilizing social media platforms to share personal experiences or informative resources about PDAs can also reach a wider audience and increase awareness.

Legal Considerations: Understanding the legal rights and protections available to individuals with PDAs is paramount in navigating the social and legal landscapes. Familiarizing oneself with disability laws, such as the Individuals with Disabilities Education Act (IDEA) or the Americans with Disabilities Act (ADA), can help advocate for appropriate accommodations in educational or workplace settings. Seeking legal counsel or assistance from advocacy organizations specializing in disabilities can provide valuable insights into legal rights and avenues for recourse in case of discrimination or lack of accommodations.

In essence, effective advocacy and raising awareness about PDA are vital components in creating supportive environments for individuals with this unique profile. Individuals with PDA can navigate social and legal landscapes more effectively by equipping themselves with knowledge, building a strong support network, and actively engaging in advocacy efforts. Stay tuned for further insights on legal considerations, rights, and educational accommodations for individuals with PDAs as we delve deeper into empowering readers to advocate effectively.

Navigating Legal Considerations and Educational Rights for Individuals with PDA

Legal considerations, rights, and educational accommodations are crucial when supporting individuals with Pathological Demand Avoidance (PDA). Understanding PDA's legal framework can empower families and caregivers to advocate effectively for their loved ones. Educational rights are fundamental, as they ensure that individuals with PDA have access to appropriate support and accommodations in school settings. It is essential to familiarize oneself with the laws and regulations that protect the rights of individuals with disabilities, including PDA.

Individualized Education Programs (IEPs) significantly secure appropriate educational accommodations for individuals with PDA. These programs outline the specific needs of the individual and detail the support services they require to succeed academically. Working closely with school administrators and exceptional education professionals to develop a comprehensive

IEP tailored to the unique challenges of PDA is essential. Advocacy within the educational system is critical to implementing these accommodations effectively.

In addition to educational considerations, being aware of legal rights that protect individuals with PDA in various contexts is vital. Understanding anti-discrimination laws, such as the Americans with Disabilities Act (ADA) and Section 504 of the Rehabilitation Act, can help ensure that individuals with PDA are not discriminated against in employment, housing, or public services. These laws provide a framework for advocating for reasonable accommodations and ensuring equal access to opportunities for individuals with disabilities.

Navigating the legal landscape can be complex, but there are resources available to support families and caregivers in advocating for individuals with PDAs. Legal advocacy organizations specializing in disability rights can guide and assist in understanding and asserting legal rights. These organizations can offer valuable insights into navigating legal processes and advocating effectively for individuals with PDAs in various settings.

When seeking educational accommodations or asserting legal rights on behalf of individuals with PDA, it is essential to approach discussions with a clear understanding of their needs and challenges. Effective communication is critical when advocating for accommodations or asserting legal rights, as it helps ensure that all parties involved understand the situation comprehensively. By clearly articulating the specific needs of individuals with PDA and providing relevant information about the condition, families and caregivers can increase the likelihood of securing appropriate support.

Empowering individuals with PDA involves understanding their unique challenges and advocating for their rights and access to necessary accommodations. Families and caregivers can navigate the social and legal landscapes more effectively by familiarizing themselves with educational rights, legal considerations, and available advocacy resources. Taking proactive steps to secure appropriate support and accommodations can make a significant difference in the lives of individuals with PDA, enabling them to thrive academically, professionally, and socially.

Navigating social situations and public perceptions and advocating effectively for individuals with Pathological Demand Avoidance (PDA) requires a strategic approach that empowers the individual with PDA and their support system. Understanding individuals' unique challenges with PDA is essential in fostering a supportive environment that encourages their growth and development. One can navigate social landscapes more effectively by equipping oneself with knowledge and practical strategies.

Building Awareness: One of the first steps in advocacy is raising awareness about PDAs. Educating others about the condition can help dispel misconceptions and promote understanding. By sharing personal experiences, insights, and resources, individuals can contribute to a more inclusive and informed society. Utilizing social media platforms, local communities, and educational institutions can effectively raise awareness about PDAs and advocate for more significant support.

Challenging Misconceptions: Addressing misconceptions surrounding PDA is crucial in advocating for individuals with the condition. Many people may not fully understand the complexities of PDA, leading to stigma or misinterpretation of behaviors. Advocates can challenge stereotypes and promote acceptance and empathy by providing accurate information, correcting misunderstandings, and sharing real-life stories.

Effective Communication: Communication is vital in navigating social situations for individuals with PDAs. Developing clear communication strategies tailored to the individual's needs can help mitigate misunderstandings and conflicts. Visual aids, social stories, or role-playing scenarios can enhance communication skills and facilitate smoother interactions in various settings.

Collaborative Advocacy: Working collaboratively with educators, healthcare professionals, employers, and community members is essential in advocating for individuals with PDAs. Building solid partnerships based on mutual respect and shared goals can lead to more effective support systems and accommodations. By advocating together as a team, advocates can amplify their voices and create positive change within their communities.

Legal Rights and Accommodations: Understanding the legal rights and accommodations available for individuals with PDA is crucial in advocating for their needs. Familiarizing oneself with relevant laws, policies, and resources can empower advocates to secure necessary support in educational settings, workplaces, or public spaces. Seeking guidance from legal professionals or advocacy organizations can provide valuable insights into navigating legal landscapes effectively.

Empowering Self-Advocacy: Empowering individuals with PDA to advocate for themselves is critical to promoting independence and self-determination. Encouraging self-advocacy skills such as self-expression, assertiveness, and problem-solving can help individuals navigate social challenges autonomously. Providing self-advocacy training or mentorship opportunities can further enhance their ability to communicate their needs effectively.

The journey through advocacy and awareness for PDA is both necessary and empowering. By embracing effective advocacy strategies, you become a voice for those who might struggle to articulate their own needs. It's crucial to remember that raising awareness is about disseminating information and fostering understanding and empathy within communities.

Legal considerations and rights ensure that individuals with PDA receive the support and accommodations they need, especially in educational settings. Knowing these rights is not just beneficial—it's transformative. It equips you with the tools to advocate for necessary changes that can significantly enhance the life and learning experiences of someone with PDA.

Navigating social situations can often be challenging. However, with the right strategies, altering public perceptions and encouraging a more inclusive environment becomes possible. Your role as an advocate involves speaking up and educating others, creating a ripple effect that promotes broader societal acceptance.

Take action today by applying the simple yet effective strategies discussed. Whether initiating conversations, utilizing legal channels, or setting up supportive educational frameworks, your involvement can bring about real change. Remember, every small step contributes to a more significant movement toward acceptance and understanding.

Your advocacy uplifts individuals with PDA and enriches their lives with deeper connections and insights. So, continue to learn, share, and grow in your journey. The path of advocacy you've embarked on is one of profound impact—keep moving forward with confidence and determination.

Chapter 14: Looking Ahead: The Future of PDA Research and Support

"Individuals with PDA possess unique strengths and

perspectives that, when nurtured, can lead

to remarkable achievements."

Unknown

Envisioning Tomorrow: The Evolution of PDA Insight and Intervention

The realm of Pathological Demand Avoidance (PDA) has long been cloaked in misunderstanding and insufficient research, leaving those affected by this profile within the autism spectrum often grappling with inadequate support systems. However, as we stand on the precipice of discoveries and methodologies in autism research, there is burgeoning hope for significant advancements in how we understand, interact with, and support individuals with PDA. This chapter delves into the future possibilities that can transform lives by enhancing the therapeutic landscape and fostering robust support networks.

The current state of PDA research reveals a critical need for more profound, more nuanced studies that go beyond surface symptoms to understand PDA's root causes and manifestations. The promise of future research lies in its potential to unveil tailored therapeutic approaches that align closely with the unique needs of those with PDAs. Researchers and practitioners can offer more effective interventions by focusing on individualized strategies rather than one-size-fits-all solutions.

Integrating technology in therapy has opened new avenues for customized support systems. Innovations such as AI-driven behavioral analysis and virtual reality simulations could revolutionize therapy sessions, making them more accessible and less stressful for individuals with PDAs. These technological advancements aim to improve the quality of therapeutic interventions and ensure they are widely accessible.

Community involvement and support networks play a pivotal role in shaping a supportive ecosystem for individuals with PDA and their families. Encouraging active participation in online forums, local groups, and national associations can provide emotional support and practical advice, creating a shared pool of resources and experiences. This collective wisdom is invaluable in crafting empathetic and effective strategies.

Looking ahead, there is an undeniable wave of optimism for new diagnostic tools that could lead to earlier and more precise identification of PDAs. Early diagnosis is crucial as it paves the way for timely intervention, setting the stage for better developmental outcomes. Furthermore, increased awareness and understanding among educators and professionals will foster more accommodating and nurturing environments for individuals with PDAs.

This chapter also highlights the importance of resilience and empowerment—qualities that are essential for both individuals with PDA and their caregivers. By adopting practices that promote these traits, families can navigate the challenges associated with PDA with greater confidence and positivity. It's about moving from a mindset of merely coping to one of thriving.

In synthesizing these themes, this chapter not only forecasts a hopeful future but also reinforces the book's overarching message: understanding PDA deeply and supporting those affected effectively requires continuous learning, adaptation, and community engagement. With concerted efforts across research, technology, community involvement, and education sectors, we can look forward to a society where individuals with PDA are supported and truly understood—a noble and attainable goal.

Advancements in PDA research, therapy, and support have the potential to significantly improve the quality of life for individuals with Pathological Demand Avoidance (PDA) and their families. Research efforts are continuously evolving, shedding light on the complexities of PDA and paving the way for more effective interventions. By staying informed about the latest findings in PDA research, individuals can better understand the condition and tailor support strategies accordingly. Therapy approaches that specifically address the unique needs of individuals with PDA are essential for fostering growth and development. These therapies can focus on building emotional regulation skills, improving social interactions, and enhancing communication abilities.

In addition to research and therapy advancements, the importance of robust support networks cannot be overstated. Connecting with others who understand the challenges of PDA can provide a sense of belonging and validation. Support groups offer a platform for sharing experiences, gaining insights, and learning from each other's strategies. Engaging with a supportive community can help individuals feel less isolated and more empowered in their journey with PDA. Moreover, these networks can serve as sources of encouragement, motivation, and practical advice for navigating daily obstacles.

While progress in PDA research is promising, it is crucial for individuals and families to actively seek out updated information and stay abreast of new developments. Therapies tailored to address the specific needs of individuals with PDA can make a significant difference in their overall well-being. Support networks are vital to understanding and solidarity, offering valuable insights and emotional sustenance.

Joining Support Networks and Communities for Understanding and Growth

In understanding and supporting Pathological Demand Avoidance (PDA), seeking involvement in support networks and communities can be a transformative step toward shared learning and growth. Navigating the complexities of PDA can be daunting, but you are not alone. Connecting with others on a similar path can offer invaluable insights, practical advice, and, most importantly, a sense of belonging in a community that understands your challenges.

Engaging with support networks opens up opportunities for shared learning. By interacting with individuals with firsthand PDA experience, you can gain new perspectives, strategies, and coping mechanisms that may resonate with your unique situation. Learning from others' journeys can provide knowledge and practical tips you may not have discovered.

Support communities offer a safe space for growth and empowerment. In these environments, you can freely express your concerns, share your triumphs, and receive encouragement from those who truly comprehend the nuances of PDA. Being part of a supportive network can foster resilience and empowerment, helping you navigate the challenges of PDA with newfound strength and confidence.

Practical solutions emerge from collective wisdom. Within these communities, you may encounter innovative approaches to managing demands, fostering positive relationships, and promoting self-care. By actively participating in discussions and sharing your experiences, you contribute to the collective knowledge base, enriching the community with your insights and gaining valuable feedback.

Taking control of your journey involves reaching out for support. Embracing the guidance and camaraderie of support networks can be a pivotal moment in your quest to understand and navigate PDA effectively. By engaging with these communities, you empower yourself to face challenges head-on, armed with the collective wisdom of those who have walked similar paths.

Remember that growth often happens in a community. Connecting with others who share your experiences and struggles creates a supportive environment where learning is reciprocal, and progress is collective. Together, you can forge ahead with newfound clarity and confidence, knowing you are part of a network that values understanding, empathy, and shared growth.

In summary, seeking involvement in support networks and communities is not just about finding help; it's about joining a collective journey toward greater understanding, resilience, and empowerment. Embrace the opportunity to connect with others who share your experiences, for within these connections lie the seeds of transformation and growth in your journey with PDA.

As we look ahead to the future of individuals with PDA, it is essential to foster a sense of hope, resilience, and empowerment within ourselves and the community around us. Hope is a beacon, guiding us through challenging times and reminding us that brighter days are on the horizon. It is crucial to hold onto this hope, knowing that progress is possible even in adversity.

Resilience is a powerful trait that enables individuals with PDA to bounce back from setbacks and continue their journey toward growth and understanding. By cultivating resilience within ourselves and those we support, we can navigate the complexities of PDA with greater strength and determination. Through resilience, we can overcome obstacles and emerge stronger on the other side.

Empowerment plays a crucial role in shaping the future of individuals with PDAs. By empowering ourselves and others with knowledge, skills, and support, we can create environments where individuals with PDA can thrive. Empowerment allows us to take control of our circumstances, advocate for our needs, and foster understanding within our communities.

In the journey towards supporting individuals with PDAs, it is crucial to remember that every step forward contributes to a brighter future for all, no matter how small. Each action to enhance understanding, support, and promote acceptance brings us closer to a more inclusive and compassionate society where individuals with PDAs can shine.

By embracing open-mindedness and flexibility, we can adapt to the unique needs of individuals with PDAs and create supportive environments that nurture their strengths. Through this adaptability, we can break down barriers, challenge misconceptions, and pave the way for a future where individuals with PDA are valued for their unique perspectives and contributions.

As we progress on this journey of growth and discovery, let us hold onto the pillars of hope, resilience, and empowerment. These qualities will guide us through challenges, inspire us to keep pushing forward, and remind us of the incredible potential within each individual with PDA. Together, we can create a future where all individuals are seen, heard, and supported in their journey towards fulfillment and success.

As we reach the end of our exploration into the world of Pathological Demand Avoidance, we are poised at a promising threshold. The potential advancements in PDA research, therapy, and support we have discussed offer a roadmap to more effective and empathetic ways to engage with individuals navigating this complex profile. These advancements are theoretical and critical to transformative practices that significantly improve lives.

The encouragement to participate in support networks and communities cannot be overstated. Shared learning and growth foster an environment where strategies and experiences are exchanged, enhancing the support system for everyone involved. This is a dynamic process—one that enriches both the giver and the receiver. By engaging with these communities, you are receiving support and contributing to the broader knowledge and understanding of PDA.

Lastly, embracing hope, resilience, and empowerment as foundational elements in the journey with PDA is essential. These are not just aspirational concepts but practical approaches that can guide daily interactions and long-term planning. They enable us to see beyond immediate challenges and recognize the incredible potential of individuals with PDAs.

Embrace these insights with confidence. Each step based on this understanding helps build a more inclusive society where individuals with PDAs can thrive. Remember, the journey is personal and collective; your actions contribute to societal changes.

The path ahead is illuminated by knowledge, empathy, and action. Let us move forward with a commitment to apply what we have learned, continuously seek new knowledge, and, most importantly, support each other with compassion and understanding. Here's to a future where every individual with a PDA is recognized for their unique strengths and supported in a way that respects their individuality.

Epilogue

"The greatest challenge in life is discovering who you are.

The second greatest is being happy

with what you find."

Unknown

Embracing the Journey: A Closing Reflection

As we conclude our exploration into the intricate world of Pathological Demand Avoidance (PDA), I hope this book has illuminated a path for you that deepens your understanding and empowers you to act with compassion and competence. The journey with PDA is unique for each individual, and by embracing this uniqueness, we can transform challenges into opportunities for growth and connection.

This book has aimed to bridge the gap between confusion and clarity, providing you with the knowledge and tools necessary to support individuals with PDAs effectively. We've explored the nuances of demand avoidance, delved into the emotional world of those affected by PDA, and uncovered strategies that honor their strengths while accommodating their needs.

Real-world applications of this understanding are vast. Whether you are a parent seeking to navigate daily interactions with your child, an educator striving to create an inclusive classroom, or a therapist designing interventions that resonate with your clients, the insights from this book are designed to be directly applicable. They offer a starting point for conversations, adjustments in approaches, and, most importantly, a shift in perspective that recognizes the potential in every individual with PDA.

To recap the main ideas: We discussed the importance of recognizing PDA as more than just a series of behaviors but as a distinct profile within the autism spectrum that requires specialized understanding. We emphasized strategies such as flexibility, negotiation, and collaboration over traditional methods of authority and demand. We highlighted the significance of emotional regulation and relationship-building as foundational elements in supporting individuals with PDAs.

In applying these insights, I urge you to start small. Choose one strategy that resonates with you and implement it consistently. Observe its impact and adjust as needed. Change often comes incrementally, and every step forward is a victory worth celebrating.

While this book strives to provide comprehensive guidance, it is essential to acknowledge its limitations. Each individual with a PDA is unique, and what works for one may not work for another. Therefore, further research into personalized approaches and long-term outcomes remains essential. Your experiences and feedback as readers can contribute significantly to this ongoing exploration.

I encourage you to take what you've learned here and use it as a foundation for further discovery. Engage with communities, participate in discussions, and continue your education on this complex topic. Let's keep pushing the boundaries of what we know so that we can better serve those who live with PDAs.

I leave you with hope and determination as we part ways in this literary journey. You possess the tools needed to make meaningful changes in your lives and the lives of those affected by PDA. Let's embrace these challenges not just with knowledge but also with heart.

"The only real voyage of discovery consists not

in seeking new landscapes but in

having new eyes."

Marcel Proust

This quote beautifully encapsulates our journey through understanding PDA—not just learning about new strategies but seeing our loved ones through new eyes of understanding, empathy, and empowerment.

Conclusion

"Empathy is the lovefire of sweet remembrance

and shared understanding."

John Eaton

As we reach the closing pages of our exploration into the realm of PDA, we must reflect on the distance we've traveled together. Through the chapters, we've embarked on a profound investigation into the lives of individuals with Pathological Demand Avoidance, uncovering the nuances of their experiences, the challenges they face, and their immense potential. This concluding chapter aims to encapsulate the essence of our collective journey, reaffirming the core messages and inspiring further action.

First and foremost, it's crucial to acknowledge that understanding PDA is not a destination but a continuous process. The landscapes of neurodiversity are vast and varied, and as we deepen our knowledge, we must remain open to learning, adapting, and evolving our perspectives. The stories and strategies shared within these pages are a gateway to a much richer dialogue on how society can better accommodate and champion the needs and strengths of those with PDAs.

A pivotal theme that is woven through this narrative is the power of empathy and acceptance. Recognizing the unique worldviews and experiences of individuals with PDA is the first step in advocating for change. This demands tolerance and a genuine effort to understand and meet these individuals where they are, creating spaces where their voices are heard and valued.

Equally, we have stressed the importance of flexibility in both thought and action. Traditional approaches to support and intervention often fall short when applied to the complex dynamics of PDA. Thus, we must champion innovative practices prioritizing the individual's autonomy, interests, and well-being, fostering environments where they can thrive on their terms.

The role of community and collaborative support networks has emerged as a lighthouse guiding the way. Within the stories of families, educators, and professionals lies the testament to what can be achieved when we unite in our efforts. Sharing experiences, resources, and strategies enriches the collective pool of knowledge, ensuring no one has to navigate these waters alone.

Looking ahead, the path is lined with both challenges and opportunities. It's an invitation to each of us—whether directly affected by PDA or not—to contribute to a more inclusive, understanding, and compassionate world. The dialogues initiated here must continue beyond the confines of these pages in homes, schools, workplaces, and communities.

In conclusion, as we part ways, carry forward the message that at the heart of all our discussions, strategies, and stories are individuals—each with their dreams, struggles, and aspirations. Recognizing, celebrating, and nurturing this individuality is not just the responsibility of those touched by PDA but a collective societal duty. The voyage of discovery may be complex, but the diverse tapestry of human experience undeniably enriches it.

- Empathy and Understanding: Strive to see the world through the eyes of those with PDA.
- Flexibility in Approaches: Abandon one-size-fits-all solutions for personalized, adaptable strategies.
- Celebration of Strengths: Focus on the capabilities and potential of individuals with PDAs rather than just the challenges.
- Building Community: Engage with and contribute to support networks sharing knowledge and resources.
- Ongoing Education: Commit to continuous learning and advocacy to promote wider societal acceptance and accommodation.
- Action for Inclusion: Implement inclusive practices in all areas of life to support the genuine integration of individuals with PDAs.

The voyage may have concluded within these pages, but understanding, supporting, and advocating for individuals with PDAs is just beginning.

Bonus Material

Your Questions, Answered!

1. How Can Parents Initially Identify Signs of PDA in Their Children?

Identifying signs of Pathological Demand Avoidance (PDA) in children can be complex due to the condition's nuanced nature. Parents and caregivers must closely observe their children's behavior patterns, especially their responses to everyday demands. Unlike typical tantrums or stubbornness seen in children, those with PDA may exhibit extreme stress, anxiety, or avoidance strategies when faced with ordinary requests or expectations. This behavior is rooted in an overwhelming need to control their environment and avoid demands that trigger anxiety, not in willful defiance.

Early signs of PDA might include the child employing social strategies to avoid demands, such as distraction, making excuses, or negotiating. For instance, a child might suddenly become 'physically incapacitated' with an ailment when asked to clean their room or do homework, only to recover swiftly once the demand is removed. Unlike typical childhood evasion, these strategies are more elaborate and consistently applied to avoid various needs, including those involving activities the child usually enjoys.

Parents might also notice that their child exhibits an unusually intense level of comfort with fantasy or role-play, often preferring to remain in these make-believe scenarios rather than engage with real-world tasks. While imaginative play is a healthy part of development, children with PDA might use it as a tool to escape from realities they find distressing or demanding.

Social interactions can also serve as a clue. Children with PDA often struggle with forming and maintaining friendships. They may find the social demands of play and cooperation particularly challenging, leading to isolation or peer conflicts. However, it's important to note that these children can be delightful on their terms, often showing great empathy and insight in comfortable, non-demanding environments.

Recognizing these signs early on enables parents to seek appropriate support and interventions tailored to their child's needs. Diagnosing PDA is a multidisciplinary effort requiring professional insight from psychologists, psychiatrists, and educational specialists. Understanding and identifying PDA is the first step towards creating an effective support system that can help the child develop coping mechanisms, manage anxiety, and lead a fulfilling life. Engaging with professionals knowledgeable about PDAs and their management is crucial for parents navigating this challenging yet manageable path.

2. What Are the Key Differences Between PDA and Other Forms of Autism?

Pathological Demand Avoidance (PDA) is a behavior profile within the autism spectrum that is characterized by an individual's extreme avoidance of everyday demands and expectations, rooted in high anxiety levels rather than intentional defiance. This condition distinguishes itself from other forms of autism through its unique set of behaviors and the underlying anxiety that drives it. Individuals with PDA deploy a range of strategies to avoid demands, which can be more sophisticated than those typically seen in individuals with other forms of autism. These strategies include social manipulation, delay tactics, and withdrawal into fantasy.

Unlike other forms of autism, where difficulties with social communication and interaction are prominent, individuals with PDA might appear socially adept in controlled or preferred circumstances. However, this social adaptability serves primarily to manage their environment and avoid demands rather than to foster genuine social connections. Their comfort with role-play and fantasy can often mask their difficulties navigating real-world interactions and complying with external expectations. This can lead observers to misinterpret the challenges faced by those with PDA, overlooking the profound anxiety and need for autonomy driving their behavior.

The core difference between PDA and other forms of autism lies in how anxiety is triggered and managed. For someone with a

PDA, the mere perception of an external demand or requirement—regardless of its nature—can trigger an overwhelming anxiety response. This includes activities they might typically enjoy or tasks that seem trivial to others. The intensity and unpredictability of these anxiety responses necessitate a tailored approach to support and intervention. Traditional autism support strategies that rely on structure, predictability, and routine can often exacerbate feelings of anxiety in individuals with PDA, making it crucial for parents, educators, and professionals to adopt more flexible, individualized strategies that prioritize the person's need for control and autonomy.

Understanding and differentiating PDA from other forms of autism is vital for providing adequate support and interventions. It requires a nuanced approach that recognizes the pervasive anxiety at the heart of the condition, emphasizing patience, flexibility, and creativity in response strategies. Recognizing the distinct nature of PDA not only aids in creating a supportive and understanding environment for individuals with the condition but also enriches our comprehension of the autism spectrum as a whole. By prioritizing the unique needs and behaviors of individuals with PDA, we can help them manage anxiety, engage more freely with the world on their terms, and lead fulfilling lives.

3. How Can Teachers Adapt Classroom Environments to Better Support Students With Pda?

Adapting classroom environments to support students with Pathological Demand Avoidance (PDA) requires a nuanced understanding of the condition and a willingness to implement personalized, flexible strategies that cater to the individual's need for control and autonomy. One crucial adaptation is creating a low-demand environment that minimizes triggers of anxiety. This can be achieved by offering choices whenever possible, allowing the student to exercise some degree of control over their activities, thereby reducing perceived demands. Teachers might present tasks as suggestions rather than directives, use indirect requests, or offer multiple options for how and when work can be completed. Such an approach helps mitigate students' anxiety around demands and encourages voluntary task engagement.

Additionally, the classroom setting should be adapted to provide a safe and comfortable space that acknowledges the student's sensory preferences and need for escape routes when overwhelmed. Sensory sensitivities are common among individuals on the autism spectrum, including those with PDA. Providing a sensory-friendly classroom with areas where students can retreat to when feeling anxious or overwhelmed can be particularly beneficial. This could include quiet zones, areas with dimmed lighting, or corners dedicated to relaxation and decompression. Teachers can also incorporate flexible seating arrangements and allow for movement breaks, recognizing that students with PDA may struggle to remain seated and attentive for prolonged periods.

Incorporating interests and using motivational techniques tailored to the individual's preferences foster engagement and participation. Since students with PDA may show greater involvement and motivation when tasks are aligned with their interests, educators should integrate these interests into the curriculum wherever possible. Furthermore, building a positive, supportive relationship is paramount. Teachers should strive to establish trust and understanding, emphasizing empathy and patience rather than discipline and consequences. This entails recognizing the anxiety-driven nature of the student's behavior and avoiding punitive measures that could exacerbate their distress.

Finally, collaboration with parents, caregivers, and exceptional education professionals is vital to creating a consistent and supportive approach across different environments. Regular communication and sharing of strategies that are effective in managing the student's anxiety and avoidance behaviors can contribute significantly to their success in the classroom. Training for teachers and support staff on PDAs and their management can also aid in fostering a more inclusive and understanding educational atmosphere.

By adopting these adaptive strategies, educators can create a classroom environment that accommodates the unique needs of students with PDA and promotes their academic and social development. It emphasizes the importance of flexibility, understanding, and individualized approaches in education, contributing to a more inclusive and supportive learning experience for all students.

4. What Strategies Can Professionals Employ to Encourage Cooperation From Individuals With PDAs without Triggering Their Demand Avoidance?

Encouraging cooperation from individuals with Pathological Demand Avoidance (PDA) without triggering their avoidance behaviors necessitates a profound understanding of the condition and a strategic, empathetic approach. The primary goal is to frame tasks and demands in a way that reduces perceived pressure, making the individual feel more in control of the situation. Professionals, such as therapists, educators, and healthcare providers, can employ various techniques to achieve this delicate balance. Key among these strategies is the use of indirect language and offering choices, which can significantly lower the individual's anxiety related to demands. For instance, instead of giving direct commands, a professional might present options or use a more collaborative language, asking for help or suggesting an activity as a game.

Furthermore, leveraging the individual's interests is a potent strategy to encourage engagement and cooperation. Activities and requests that align with their preferences or fascinations can naturally motivate individuals with PDA, as their engagement drives their willingness to participate. This approach not only bypasses the stress associated with direct demands but also fosters a positive, rewarding environment that acknowledges their needs and interests. Professionals must invest time in understanding what motivates the person with PDA, as this knowledge can be instrumental in designing effective interventions or educational plans.

To cultivate a successful interaction with individuals with PDA, creating an atmosphere of trust and respect is essential. This involves recognizing and validating their feelings, especially their anxiety around demands, without judgment. Strategies such as providing clear and consistent explanations for why specific tasks are necessary and ensuring a predictable environment to the greatest extent possible can help reduce anxiety. Professionals should also be flexible in their approaches, ready to adjust or retract demands if they're causing distress, and always look for overwhelming signs. Collaboration with the individual to find mutually agreeable solutions reinforces their autonomy and reduces the propensity for avoidance behaviors.

Lastly, praise and positive reinforcement are crucial in encouraging cooperation from individuals with PDA. However small, acknowledging their efforts and successes can build confidence and resilience. It's essential, however, that praise is genuine and not seen as another form of demand or expectation, which could counteract the intended positive effects.

By integrating these approaches, professionals can create more effective and supportive strategies to engage individuals with PDAs. This not only aids in reducing the frequency and intensity of demand-avoidant behaviors but also supports the individual's overall well-being and development.

5. What Role Do Genetics and Environment Play in the Development of PDA?

The interplay between genetics and environment in the development of Pathological Demand Avoidance (PDA) is a complex and nuanced topic, capturing the interest of researchers and professionals in psychology and developmental disorders. While the exact cause of PDA remains unclear, evidence suggests that a combination of genetic predispositions and environmental factors plays a significant role in the manifestation of this condition.

Genetics, on the one hand, may contribute to the development of PDA through hereditary transmission of traits associated with autism spectrum disorders, given that some consider PDA as part of this spectrum. Although specific genes related to PDA have not been conclusively identified, studies in autism and related neurodevelopmental disorders indicate that genetic variations can influence the likelihood of developing these conditions. These genetic factors may predispose an individual to exhibit behaviors characteristic of PDA, such as the intense avoidance of everyday demands and anxiety in response to expectations.

Environmental factors also play a critical role in shaping the expression of these genetic predispositions into the distinct patterns of behaviors observed in PDA. Early childhood experiences, parenting styles, trauma, and stress levels can all influence the severity and presentation of the condition. For instance, a nurturing environment that allows for adaptation and coping mechanisms may mitigate some of the challenges associated with PDA. In contrast, a highly structured or stressful environment might exacerbate avoidance behaviors. Furthermore, social influences, including interactions with peers and educational settings, can impact the development and management of PDA, highlighting the importance of supportive and understanding environments.

In sum, the development of PDA is likely the result of an intricate interplay between genetic predispositions and environmental experiences. This multifactorial perspective underscores the necessity for a comprehensive approach to assessing, understanding, and supporting individuals with PDAs. Recognizing the contribution of genetics and environment can guide more effective interventions and support mechanisms tailored to the needs of each individual with PDA, facilitating their ability to engage more fully with the world around them.

6. How Can Families Advocate for the Needs of a Member With PDA within the Broader Community or School System?

Advocating for a family member with Pathological Demand Avoidance (PDA) within the broader community or school system is crucial for their development and well-being. It requires a multifaceted approach that begins with education and awareness. Families must first ensure they thoroughly understand PDA, including its characteristics, challenges, and strategies to support individuals facing these challenges. With this knowledge, families can educate those within the community and school systems, often starting with teachers, administrators, and support staff. This educational endeavor might involve sharing resources, organizing training sessions with PDA experts, or simply discussing the specific needs and optimal support strategies for the individual with a PDA.

Building a robust and collaborative relationship with the school system is another pillar of effective advocacy. This involves open, regular communication and planning meetings that include the family educators and other relevant professionals such as therapists and counselors who understand PDA well. Creating an Individualized Education Plan (IEP) or a similar personalized plan that outlines accommodations, strategies, and goals specific to the individual's needs is essential. These plans should emphasize the use of flexible and adaptable approaches to learning, acknowledging the unique ways in which people with PDA engage with education and social interactions. It's also vital for these plans to include strategies for managing anxiety and demand avoidance in a school setting, with input from the individual with a PDA whenever possible.

Furthermore, advocating within the broader community may involve raising awareness and seeking support beyond the educational sphere. This could include local clubs, sports teams, or other extracurricular activities where inclusivity and accommodations must be negotiated and implemented. Engaging local media, social media platforms, or community forums can also raise public awareness and understanding of PDA, potentially fostering a more supportive environment. Lastly, networking with other families who have members with PDA can provide mutual support, share effective strategies, and collectively advocate for systemic changes or resources in the community and education systems that cater to the needs of individuals with PDA.

By taking these steps, families can play a pivotal role in ensuring that their loved ones with PDAs receive the understanding, acceptance, and support they need, both in educational settings and within the community. This advocacy is about securing accommodations or modifications and fostering a society that values and includes all individuals, recognizing the diverse ways in which people experience and interact with the world around them.

7. What Are the Most Effective Therapeutic Approaches for Managing PDA, and How Do They Differ From Those Used With Other Asd Conditions?

The most effective therapeutic approaches for managing Pathological Demand Avoidance (PDA) place a strong emphasis on flexibility, collaboration, and understanding the individual's specific needs. Unlike traditional therapeutic approaches often applied in Autism Spectrum Disorders (ASDs) that might focus heavily on structured interventions and behavior modification techniques, therapies for individuals with PDA prioritize strategies that reduce anxiety around demands and encourage voluntary cooperation. This nuanced approach is predicated on respecting the person's autonomy and employing indirect methods of engagement, such as offering choices and using a more playful or engaging style to motivate participation in activities or tasks.

One of the critical therapeutic approaches for PDA is the use of a collaborative and flexible method, often seen in therapies such as cognitive behavioral therapy (CBT), which has been adapted to meet the needs of someone with PDA. These adaptations might include a greater focus on developing strategies for managing anxiety and reducing the situational pressures that trigger demand avoidance behaviors. Therapists might work with individuals to identify specific demand triggers and develop personalized coping mechanisms to handle these situations more effectively, ensuring that the methods resonate with the individual's preferences and comfort levels.

Another critical approach involves using creative and engaging strategies, such as role-play or gamification, to encourage learning and growth. This can help circumvent the individual's resistance to direct demands by embedding learning and development opportunities in activities they perceive as enjoyable or exciting. Furthermore, fostering an environment where choices are plentiful and autonomy is respected can significantly reduce the stress associated with demands, lowering instances of avoidance behavior.

Additionally, for individuals with PDA, incorporating positive reinforcement and emotional support within therapy sessions is crucial. This builds a stronger therapist-client relationship and supports the development of self-esteem and self-awareness, empowering individuals to recognize their patterns of behavior and become more proactive in managing their responses to demands. This aspect of therapy is vital in distinguishing it from approaches used with other ASD conditions, where the emphasis might be more on compliance and adhering to established routines.

In summary, the therapeutic management of PDA requires a holistic, flexible, and individual-centered approach, significantly differing from traditional ASD therapies by prioritizing the reduction of anxiety related to demands and fostering voluntary engagement over compliance. Therapies adapted for PDA leverage understanding, collaboration, creativity, and emotional support to empower individuals, enabling them to navigate their unique challenges more effectively.

8. Can Adults Be Diagnosed With PDA, and if So, How Does the Diagnostic Process Differ From That for Children?

Yes, adults can indeed be diagnosed with Pathological Demand Avoidance (PDA), although the diagnostic process can differ significantly from that for children. This difference primarily stems from the fact that, by adulthood, individuals may have developed a complex array of coping mechanisms and strategies to mask or manage their symptoms. Additionally, the diagnostic criteria and methods used by professionals may need to be adjusted to reflect the different contexts and expectations placed on adults compared to children.

The diagnostic process for adults first involves a thorough assessment of the individual's life history, including developmental milestones, school experiences, social and employment histories, and any previous diagnoses or interventions. This comprehensive approach is essential to differentiate PDA from other conditions that might present with similar features in adulthood, such as anxiety disorders, personality disorders, or other forms of autism. Professionals, often psychologists or psychiatrists specializing in neurodevelopmental conditions, may use interviews, questionnaires, and observation methods tailored to explore the nuanced ways PDA presents in adults.

Critical to this process is understanding the individual's behavior patterns over time, especially those related to demand avoidance, social interaction, and responses to stress. The diagnostic evaluation for PDA in adults will examine how these behaviors have impacted the person's functioning across different areas of life, such as relationships, education, work, and daily living skills. Specialists will also consider the adaptive strategies the person has developed, acknowledging the challenges and the strengths that have enabled the individual to cope with their condition.

Additionally, the process involves collecting information from multiple sources, such as family members, partners, or close friends, to gain a comprehensive view of the individual's behaviors and how they have adapted over time. This multi-informant approach can help build a fuller picture of the person's life and how much PDA affects their day-to-day existence.

In summary, diagnosing PDA in adults requires a nuanced, personalized approach that accounts for the complex interplay of symptoms, coping mechanisms, and the individual's life experiences. Unlike the more straightforward diagnostic criteria often applied to children, assessing adults for PDA involves considering the lifelong trajectory of their symptoms and how they have navigated the demands of the adult world. This process not only helps affirm a diagnosis but also guides the development of effective, tailored interventions and support strategies.

9. How Does Pda Affect Social Relationships and Friendships, and What Strategies Can Help Foster Positive Interactions?

Pathological Demand Avoidance (PDA) can significantly impact social relationships and friendships, often leading to complex and multifaceted challenges. Individuals with PDA may experience intense anxiety and stress in situations that make demands on them, including social interactions, which, by their nature, can be unpredictable and demanding. This can result in behaviors aimed at avoiding these social demands, such as withdrawing from social activities, refusing invitations, or even displaying challenging behavior to escape the situation. While protecting the individual from immediate stress, these mechanisms can inadvertently lead to isolation, misunderstanding by others, and difficulties in forming and maintaining relationships.

The unique social strategies deployed by individuals with PDA often reflect their broader attempts to control their environment and reduce anxiety. For instance, they might prefer interactions on their own terms and avoid settings where they feel they have less control over the outcome. This can make typical social settings particularly challenging, such as parties or group outings. Furthermore, the intense need for autonomy and self-direction in people with PDA means that conventional social norms and expectations can feel overly restrictive and provoke anxiety, leading to avoidance.

To foster positive interactions and relationships, it's crucial to adapt approaches that respect the individual's need for control and reduce demand-related anxiety. Strategies might include allowing the person with PDA to take the lead in deciding the timing, setting, and activity for social interactions, thereby giving them a sense of control and predictability. Additionally, open and understanding communication about the individual's needs and feelings can help friends and family members recognize and respond to situations that may trigger anxiety or avoidance behaviors. For example, explaining the concept of PDA to peers and educators can foster an environment of empathy and accommodation where the individual feels supported and understood.

Creating low-demand environments and utilizing indirect requests or suggestions rather than direct demands can facilitate positive social interactions. This approach reduces the likelihood of triggering the individual's avoidance mechanisms, making social engagement less stressful and more enjoyable. Therapeutic interventions might focus on developing coping strategies for managing anxiety in social situations, improving the understanding of social cues, and gradually increasing tolerance for social demands in a supportive and controlled manner. Support groups and peer networks for individuals with PDA and their families can provide a vital source of understanding and connection, offering a safe space for social interaction without the typical demands of everyday social settings.

In summary, navigating social relationships and friendships with PDA requires a nuanced and adaptive approach, both from the individuals themselves and from those around them. Understanding and accommodating the unique challenges faced by those with PDA makes it possible to develop strategies that support meaningful and fulfilling social interactions. This involves creating environments where demands are minimized, autonomy is respected, and open communication is prioritized, ultimately enabling individuals with PDA to engage with social settings in a comfortable and enriching way.

10. What Are the Long-Term Outlooks for Individuals With PDA in Terms of Independence, Employment, and Quality of Life?

The long-term outlook for individuals with Pathological Demand Avoidance (PDA) varies significantly from one person to another, influenced by a spectrum of factors, including the severity of the condition, the support systems in place, and the coping mechanisms the individual develops over time. Independence, employment, and quality of life for those with PDA can see vast improvements with early diagnosis, tailored support, and strategies to enhance their adaptive skills and minimize stress related to demands.

Independence for individuals with PDA can be challenging due to the anxiety and avoidance behaviors associated with everyday demands and expectations. Success in this area often hinges on personalized strategies that consider the person's anxieties and triggers. Educational and therapeutic interventions tailored to the unique needs of individuals with PDA, focusing on flexibility, creativity, and the development of executive function skills, can significantly enhance their capability to manage daily tasks and responsibilities. Furthermore, support in adult life, such as occupational therapy and supported living arrangements, can provide the scaffolding needed to achieve greater independence.

Employment poses another set of challenges and opportunities for individuals with PDA. The traditional workplace's inherent demands and social interactions can be overwhelming. However, employment opportunities that offer flexibility, autonomy, and a supportive environment can lead to successful careers for many with PDAs. Employers and colleagues who understand PDA and can provide accommodations, such as flexible schedules, work-from-home options, and tailored job roles, can significantly contribute to a positive employment outcome. Vocational training and employment support tailored to the individual's interests and strengths can also facilitate meaningful career paths.

Quality of life for those with PDA is intrinsically linked to the understanding and support they receive from family, educators, healthcare providers, and society at large. A comprehensive approach that includes education about PDA, social support systems, therapeutic interventions, and accommodations in educational and employment settings can significantly improve well-being. Engagement in community activities, hobbies, and interests that align with the person's strengths and preferences can also enhance their life satisfaction and sense of belonging.

In sum, the long-term outlook for individuals with PDA involves a dynamic interplay between their abilities, the strategies they develop to cope with their challenges, and the support they receive from their environment. With concerted efforts to build a supportive and understanding framework around individuals with PDA, there is considerable potential for them to lead fulfilling lives characterized by meaningful social relationships, satisfying employment, and a high degree of independence.

11.   How Can Siblings of Individuals With Pda Understand and Cope With the Unique Challenges Their Family Faces?

Siblings of individuals with Pathological Demand Avoidance (PDA) play a unique and crucial role in the family dynamics. They may experience a range of emotions and challenges, from feelings of neglect due to the increased attention their sibling with PDA requires to confusion and frustration over their sibling's behavior and the family's different responses to it. Understanding and coping with these challenges necessitates a multifaceted approach that includes open communication, education, and emotional support tailored to the needs of these siblings.

Firstly, parents and caregivers need to foster an environment of open and age-appropriate communication with siblings of individuals with PDAs. This involves explaining the nature of PDA in understandable terms, discussing the reasons behind their sibling's behavior, and the rationale for any different treatments or expectations set by the parents. Such conversations can help demystify the sibling's condition, reducing misunderstandings and resentment. Additionally, creating opportunities for siblings to express their feelings and concerns and ensuring they feel heard and valued is critical in preventing feelings of neglect or secondary importance.

Educational interventions can further aid siblings in understanding PDA. Workshops, informational resources, and involvement in therapy sessions can equip them with knowledge about the condition and strategies to engage positively with their sibling. This strengthens the sibling relationship and provides a sense of empowerment and control over potentially challenging situations. Furthermore, involvement in support groups—either in person or online—can offer siblings a platform to meet others in similar circumstances, fostering a supportive community where they can share experiences and coping strategies.

To mitigate the impacts of living with a sibling with a PDA, families can benefit from implementing structured routines that incorporate dedicated one-on-one time for each child, ensuring siblings without PDAs feel recognized and valued. Family counseling or therapy can also be vital in addressing complex emotions and dynamics within the family unit, guiding members toward healthier interactions and mutual understanding.

In conclusion, navigating the unique challenges faced by siblings of individuals with PDA requires a balanced approach that emphasizes education, communication, and emotional support. By acknowledging the impact of PDA on all family members and adopting tailored strategies to support each child's needs, families can cultivate a more vital, more understanding environment that benefits both the individual with PDA and their siblings. This focused attention on sibling relationships and family dynamics holds the promise of fostering more harmonious relationships and a supportive family atmosphere, which is crucial for the well-being of every family member.

12.   In What Ways Can Technology Be Leveraged to Assist Individuals With PDA in Learning and Communication?

Technology can significantly enhance the learning and communication experiences of individuals with Pathological Demand Avoidance (PDA), utilizing tools and applications designed to cater to their unique needs and preferences. Digital platforms and software can be particularly effective in creating a less direct, demand-free environment where individuals with PDAs can explore and learn at their own pace. The customizable nature of many educational technologies allows for adapting learning materials to suit individual interests and levels of understanding, thus maintaining engagement without invoking the stress response often triggered by perceived demands.

For instance, interactive learning apps incorporating gamification elements can transform educational content into engaging and stimulating activities. These apps can adjust their difficulty levels and content according to the user's progress, ensuring that learning remains challenging but not overwhelmingly so. Visual aids, like video and animations, can further help simplify complex concepts, making them more accessible. Additionally, the autonomy given to users in navigating these platforms can help reduce the aversion to demands, as individuals with PDA can exert control over their learning environment, deciding when and what to study.

Communication technologies, such as speech-to-text software and communication apps, can also play a critical role in assisting those with PDAs. For individuals who find direct verbal communication challenging, these tools can offer alternative modes of expression, reducing anxiety and improving social interactions. Online forums and social media groups specifically designed for individuals with PDA or similar conditions can provide valuable opportunities for socialization within a supportive community, where members can share experiences and strategies free from the pressures of face-to-face communication.

In education settings, integrating technology can facilitate personalized learning plans that accommodate the needs of students with PDAs. Teachers and educators can utilize online resources and platforms to deliver curriculum content more flexibly and interactively. This can particularly benefit students who resist traditional teaching due to their demand-avoidant behavior. By leveraging technology, educators can foster an inclusive learning environment where students with PDA are empowered to participate and succeed.

Therefore, technology offers a versatile and practical set of tools for addressing some of the challenges faced by individuals with PDAs in learning and communication. By carefully selecting and implementing suitable technologies, parents, educators, and therapists can significantly enhance the educational experiences and quality of life for individuals with PDA, providing them with the skills and confidence needed to engage more fully with the world around them.

13. Are There Specific Legal Protections or Accommodations Individuals With PDA Can or Should Receive in the Educational System or Workplace?

In many countries, individuals with disabilities, including those diagnosed with Pathological Demand Avoidance (PDA), are eligible for legal protections and accommodations within the educational system and workplace to ensure equal access and opportunities. These legal frameworks are designed to recognize individuals' unique challenges with conditions like PDA and support their integration and success in these environments. The specific nature of accommodations and protections can vary significantly between different legal jurisdictions, but they generally aim to provide a more adaptable and responsive environment for individuals with PDAs.

Educational systems often have specific policies and legislation in place to guide the provision of support for students with PDAs. This could include the development of Individualized Education Programs (IEPs) or plans that tailor education to a student's particular needs, preferences, and strengths. Accommodations may range from modified teaching methods and assessment formats to providing technological aids that facilitate learning. Furthermore, educators and support staff may receive training to understand PDA better and implement strategies that minimize demand-avoidant behavior, enhancing these students' educational engagement and outcomes. Such legal requirements ensure that academic institutions provide an inclusive environment that acknowledges and caters to the diverse needs of all students.

In the workplace, legal protections typically revolve around anti-discrimination laws, reasonable accommodations, and promoting an inclusive work environment. Employers may be required to adjust the work setting or how tasks are presented and managed to help individuals with PDAs perform to their best abilities. This could include flexible working hours, tailored communication strategies, or creating a physical workspace that is less likely to trigger stress or anxiety for an employee with a PDA. The aim is to ensure that individuals with PDAs can access, remain in, and progress within the workplace equally with others. These accommodations and adjustments acknowledge the strengths and potential of individuals with PDA while mitigating the impact of their condition on their work performance and overall well-being.

Overall, the provision of legal protections and accommodations for individuals with PDAs in educational and workplace settings reflects a recognition of the importance of supporting diversity and inclusion. By adapting environments and practices to meet the needs of individuals with PDAs, educators, and employers can play a crucial role in facilitating their participation and success, ultimately contributing to a more inclusive society.

14.　　How Can Stress and Mental Health Challenges That Often Accompany PDA be Effectively Managed for Both the Individual and Their Families?

Managing the stress and mental health challenges associated with Pathological Demand Avoidance (PDA) necessitates a multifaceted approach that acknowledges both the individual's and their family's needs. Effective management strategies are crucial for mitigating the impact of PDA on daily life and ensuring the well-being of those affected. This involves a combination of therapeutic interventions, support systems, and practical adjustments to routines and environments.

For individuals with PDA, a key component of effective stress management is the implementation of personalized therapy sessions. Cognitive Behavioral Therapy (CBT) and other behavior modification therapies can be adapted to suit the unique challenges faced by individuals with PDA, offering strategies to manage anxiety and reduce demand-avoidant behaviors. Occupational therapy can also be beneficial, focusing on developing coping mechanisms for everyday tasks and demands. In addition to traditional therapies, the use of relaxation techniques such as mindfulness, meditation, and controlled breathing exercises can help individuals with PDA manage anxiety levels and emotional dysregulation.

Support for families is equally important, as the stress related to managing PDA can significantly impact all family members. Parenting programs and support groups specifically designed for families of individuals with PDA can provide crucial advice, strategies, and a sense of community. Education for family members about PDA and its effects is essential, enabling a supportive and understanding home environment. Respite care and other support services can also offer temporary relief for families, reducing caretaker burnout and facilitating a more balanced approach to care.

Furthermore, creating a structured yet flexible routine can help individuals with PDA and their families manage daily stresses. This involves establishing clear expectations while allowing room for adjustments based on the individual's current state of mind. For many families, leveraging the strengths and interests of the individuals with PDA—using these as incentives for engagement and completion of necessary tasks—can be a crucial strategy in reducing stress and promoting positive interactions.

In conclusion, managing the stress and mental health challenges associated with PDA is a complex process that requires a holistic and personalized approach. Combining therapeutic strategies, support for families, and practical adjustments can improve the quality of life for individuals with PDA and their families, fostering a supportive environment that encourages growth, learning, and well-being.

15.   What Ongoing Research is Being Conducted on PDA, and How Might It Change the Understanding or Treatment of the Condition in the Future?

Ongoing research into Pathological Demand Avoidance (PDA) is crucial for developing a deeper understanding of the condition, which can lead to advancements in treatment and support strategies for those affected. Research in this area encompasses a broad spectrum of studies, including exploring the biological, psychological, and social factors contributing to PDA development and manifestation. Such studies are essential for clarifying the distinction between PDA and other conditions within the autism spectrum, as well as identifying effective interventions explicitly tailored to the needs of individuals with PDA.

One key focus of current research is the examination of effective therapeutic interventions and educational strategies that can be employed to support individuals with PDA. This includes investigating the efficacy of standard autism spectrum disorder interventions when adapted for those with PDA, as well as developing new methods that are specifically designed to address the unique challenges posed by demand-avoidant behavior. For example, studies explore how different behavior management techniques and learning environments can impact individuals with PDA, aiming to discover the conditions under which they best thrive. These research efforts could lead to establishing best practice guidelines for educators and therapists working with individuals with PDAs.

Furthermore, emerging research is looking at PDA's physiological and neurological underpinnings, using advanced imaging techniques and genetic studies to uncover the biological basis of the condition. This line of inquiry could lead to breakthroughs in understanding the root causes of PDA, potentially opening up new avenues for treatment, such as pharmacological interventions or neurofeedback therapy.

Thank You

Thank you for dedicating your time to immerse yourself in the pages of this book. Your willingness to explore the world of PDA with an open mind and a compassionate heart is commendable and crucial to forging paths of understanding and acceptance.

We hope the insights and narratives shared have equipped you with valuable knowledge and inspired you to contribute to a society that celebrates diversity in all its forms. Moving forward, may you carry the principles of empathy, flexibility, and inclusion into your daily lives, championing change not only for those with PDAs but for the benefit of all individuals.

We can build a more understanding, accepting, and inclusive world.

www.ingramcontent.com/pod-product-compliance
Lightning Source LLC
Chambersburg PA
CBHW051256250726
48656CB00004B/1327